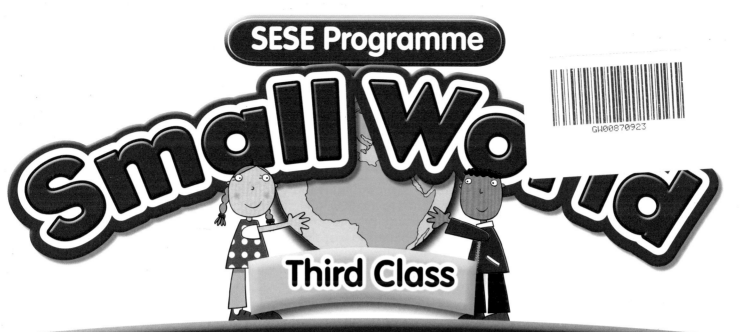

SESE Programme

Small World

Third Class

Geography & Science

CJFallon

Introduction

The fields of **Geography** and **Science** are inextricably linked. Combining the two in a Primary School textbook makes perfect sense. Enhancing this union with a complementary **History** textbook adds further value. The accompanying supplementary material and teaching ideas provide the modern teacher with fingertip access to almost everything s/he may need for the successful and enjoyable presentation of the SESE curricula. We are confident that teachers will find in *Small World* an abundance of facts, information and explorations presented in an attractive and child-friendly manner.

The *Small World* series was written by a team of **practising Primary School teachers** with a special interest in Science and Geography. It conforms to the SESE curricula and guidelines published by the NCCA. It presents the teacher with a ready-made programme of class-appropriate activities and information in an easy-to-navigate manual. Pointers to websites are provided, leading to videos, photos and other media that will be beneficial in the further exploration of topics. Throughout the series, the teacher is encouraged to devote extra time to topics of particular interest to the class. This is in keeping with the menu-driven approach of the revised SESE curricula.

Key Features:

- Strands with extensive content are covered over a two-year period. Strands with less content are covered in either 3rd class or 4th class.
- Resources are embedded in the teacher's online version of the text. This technology allows the teacher to click on a link (on an IWB, for instance) to display an internet resource that is topic-relevant.
- Science, Geography and History interlink through the 'Hot' sections in each book. The most obvious are labelled 'Hot History', 'Hot Geography' and 'Hot Science', but there are many more.
- Strands and strand units are listed at the bottom of each unit and are colour coded. Integration of Science and Geography is clearly shown.
- A glossary at the end of the book gives definitions of many new words introduced at the beginning of each unit. These words can be used in a pre-reading activity.
- The books have a range of interesting practical 'Investigate' and 'Design and Make' sections requiring few resources and not too much time. Activities and experiments should be closely supervised, and health and safety considerations should be observed.
- The textbook includes questions and activities designed to recap and revise.
- The activity book provides investigation templates and record sheets along with additional activities. Some activities have a literacy dimension to boost pupils' reading and comprehension levels.
- The teacher's manual has fortnightly schemes, a yearly scheme, integrated themes, pragmatic extension notes for each unit, answers, differentiation options, photocopiables and more.
- There is a range of assessment strategies included in the textbook and teacher's manual that link directly to the NCCA assessment guidelines, ensuring that these strategies are used in everyday teaching.

Authors: Máire Boyle, Kieran Fanning, Marie Hurley
Editor: Donna Garvin
Design and layout: Annick Doza
Illustrator: Tim Hutchinson
Photographs: Alamy; Glow Images; Thinkstock; Steve Rogers Photography; Wikimedia; Science Photo Library

ISBN 978-0-7144-1906-0

Published by
CJ Fallon
Ground Floor Block B
Liffey Valley Office Campus
Dublin 22

First edition March 2013
This reprint September 2015

© CJ Fallon

Printed in Ireland by
Turner Print Group
Earl Street
Longford

Contents

Note: The **order** in which the units appear was determined on the basis of the **literacy level** required and the difficulty of the **concept**. Naturally, the order in which the units are **taught** will be at the discretion of the teacher.

Birds of Ireland

Robin

Robin

The robin has lovely red feathers on its breast and it is not a shy bird. Robins will not allow other robins in their space. They hide their nests in trees, walls or ivy.

Blackbird

The male blackbird has a bright yellow bill (beak) and he is a beautiful singer. Female blackbirds are more brown than black! Blackbirds nest in bushes, trees, brambles or ivy.

Blackbird

Magpie

'One for sorrow, two for joy...' There were no magpies in Ireland before the year 1650 AD. Some people do not like magpies, because they take the eggs and the young of other birds. They eat creatures that have been killed on the roads by cars.

Magpie

Crow

Crow

The crow is the cleverest of birds and may even be the second smartest creature on Earth, after humans! Crows like to live near other crows in groups of nests called rookeries. A group of crows is called a murder!

Thrush

The song thrush is a wonderful singer and long ago, people used to keep thrushes in cages to enjoy their singing. They love to eat snails; they pick up a snail and crack its shell on a stone.

Thrush

Swallow

How do they do it? Their brains are the size of a pea, yet they can fly thousands of kilometres to Africa and find their way back to the exact same place in Ireland every April!

Swallow

Cuckoo

Cuckoo

The cuckoo lays her eggs in another bird's nest! Not only that, but the young cuckoos hatch early and push the other eggs and babies out of the nest in order to get all of the food.

House Sparrow

The sparrow nests under the eaves of buildings. It likes to take a dry bath by making a shallow hole in dusty ground, in which it shakes itself. The dust and grit help to get rid of any mites in its feathers.

House sparrow

Pigeon

Pigeon

The wood pigeon is wild, but some people breed homing pigeons in lofts. Homing pigeons are able to find their way home and scientists do not quite know how they do it! They were used to carry messages during wars.

Finch

Finch

There are many types of finch, including chaffinch, greenfinch and goldfinch. They are small birds and are often seen in gardens.

Wren

The wren is a very small bird and one of the few birds that builds a roof on its nest. The female lines it with feathers to make it cosy. In some parts of Ireland, people dress up in fancy dress on Saint Stephen's Day, which they call *Lá an Dreoilín*, or Wren Day.

Wren

Starling

Starlings

If you have ever seen a large flock of birds landing in a garden to eat, they were probably starlings. Aeroplanes have been known to crash after flying into a flock of starlings!

5

Unit 1: Animals and Habitats

Herbivores

Herbivores are animals that eat leaves, shoots, fruit and flowers. Elephants, pandas, sheep, cows, horses and rabbits are herbivores. Some of them have to eat all day in order to get enough food. Imagine that! Snails are herbivores. If you ever grow young plants in the garden, they might be gone the next morning because they have been eaten by snails! Giraffes are herbivores. Their long necks allow them to reach the leaves on tall trees (and to see over high walls!).

Carnivores

Think of lions, tigers, alligators and wolves. Their sharp teeth and strong jaws allow them to rip raw meat apart and to crunch bones. Most carnivores have to hunt for their food, so they are fast and strong. They will eat most other animals that they can catch, but not too many are fond of skunks! Frogs are carnivores that eat worms and insects. Eagles are carnivores with great eyesight and sharp talons (claws) for hunting small animals, birds and fish.

Omnivores

Omnivores eat plants and animals. Take birds for example: you may have seen a bird standing on one end of a worm (to hold it) while it munches the other end. The same bird might then visit a feeder for some seeds and nuts. Dogs need to be omnivores. They love to eat meat and bones and they also enjoy rice and vegetables. Most humans are omnivores. We like to eat meat and fruit and vegetables. Some people choose not to eat meat. They are called vegetarians.

What Is a Food Chain?

An earthworm eats a dead leaf. A sparrow eats the earthworm. A hawk catches the sparrow and eats it. This is an example of a food chain:

leaf ➡ worm ➡ sparrow ➡ hawk

What Do Animals Eat?

It depends on the animal. I bet you do not eat exactly the same food as the other children in your class!

- Animals that eat plants are called HERBIVORES.

- Animals that eat other animals are called CARNIVORES.

- Animals that eat both plants and animals are called OMNIVORES.

I THINK THEY'LL EAT EVERYTHING IF THEY ARE HUNGRY.

I THINK THEY'LL DIE BECAUSE THEY ARE NOT IN THE GARDEN.

I THINK THEY'LL EAT THE GREEN THINGS.

apple peels
caterpillars
leaves   grass   carrots

| **Subject:** Science | **Strand:** Living Things |
| **Strand Unit:** Plants and Animals | |

| **Subject:** Geography | **Strand:** Natural Environments |
| **Strand Unit:** The Local Natural Environment | |

Rabbits

A female rabbit is called a doe, the male is a buck and the baby is a kitten. Rabbits sleep underground in a burrow. They prefer to live in fields with dry, sandy soil or in ditches where the soil is easy to dig. They come out of their burrow to find grass to eat. They are always on their guard. They have long ears and their noses twitch. Their eyes are on the sides of their heads so that they can see all around. It is impossible to creep up on a rabbit! When the Normans came to Ireland about 850 years ago, they brought rabbits with them. Before that, there were no rabbits in Ireland.

Rabbit

Bumblebee

Bumblebees

Bumblebees are native to Ireland. This means that they have lived here for a very long time. They live in nests that they make in small holes in the ground. Bumblebees live in large families made up of a queen bee, lots of female workers and a few males. Only the female can sting, but she seldom does. Bumblebees love clover and clover loves bumblebees. The clover flower makes nectar that the bees collect. As they do so, tiny specks of pollen rub off onto them and they carry the pollen to other clover plants.

Earthworms

Very few plants would grow in Ireland if we did not have earthworms. They are herbivores. They eat leaves, roots and soil. They burrow through the soil, swallowing it and passing it through their bodies as they go. They make little tunnels that let in air and allow water to drain away. Earthworms can drown in very wet weather. That is why you may see lots of them coming up for air during very heavy rain. Earthworms do not have eyes, so they cannot see. Other creatures love to eat earthworms. They are eaten by blackbirds, thrushes, badgers and fish. That is why you will often see fishermen digging for earthworms. Some people think that if you cut an earthworm in two, each part will grow. This is not true and it is cruel. Be kind to all creatures.

Hot Science

Bumblebees do not make a lot of honey. They only make enough to feed their young.

Earthworm

Subject:	Science	Strand:	Living Things	Subject:	Geography	Strand:	Natural Environments
Strand Unit:	Plants and Animals			Strand Unit:	The Local Natural Environment		

7

Habitat: Fields and Meadows

The Corncrake

![Corncrakes]

Corncrakes

If you got two rough pieces of metal and rubbed them together, it would make an awful sound. This is like the sound made by the male corncrake. To make matters worse, he likes to sing at night! Although it is called a corncrake, this bird lives in fields and meadows with tall grass. It builds its nest on the ground. The nest is usually made of grass. The corncrake visits Ireland for the summer. It spends the winter in Africa. Sadly, the corncrake has become rare in Ireland. One of the reasons for this is that when farmers are cutting hay, they can harm the nest and the young chicks by accident. Many farmers now start to mow a field in the middle. This gives the corncrake a better chance to escape. The other reason the corncrake is rare is that many farmers prefer to cut their grass when it is short, to make silage. Long ago, most farmers preferred long grass for hay. Corncrakes cannot nest in short grass.

Meadow Brown

Common Blue

Red Admiral

Butterflies

There are 20,000 different types of butterfly in the world. Butterflies found in Ireland can be placed into four groups. (1) Small butterflies such as the Common Blue are found in fields and meadows all over the country. (2) Brown butterflies like the Meadow Brown are very common. (3) White butterflies such as the Cabbage White are not liked by gardeners, because they nibble the cabbage leaves. (4) The last group are multi-coloured butterflies, such as the Red Admiral. Adult butterflies lay their eggs on plants. When an egg hatches, the caterpillar eats the leaves of the plant. The caterpillar turns into a pupa and rests. The adult butterfly is the last stage of the life cycle.

Cabbage White

Pupa

Activities

1. Name an animal you would not have found in a meadow in Ireland a thousand years ago.
2. What type of plant do bumblebees like?
3. What can happen to an earthworm in very wet weather?
4. To which continent do corncrakes fly for the winter?
5. Where do corncrakes build their nests?
6. Name and draw the four stages in the life cycle of the butterfly.
7. Make two lists of **(a)** creatures you might find in a field in Ireland (for example, rabbit), and **(b)** creatures you would not find in a field in Ireland (for example, crab).
8. How many animal sounds can you think of? (For example, an owl hoots.)

| Subject: | Science | Strand: | Living Things | Subject: | Geography | Strand: | Natural Environments |
| Strand Unit: | Plants and Animals | | | Strand Unit: | The Local Natural Environment | | |

Habitat: The Seashore

Seabirds

Many types of bird may be seen on the seashore, such as seagulls, gannets, shags and razorbills (which look like small penguins). The biggest seagull in Ireland is the great black-backed seagull. If your school is not too far from the sea, your yard might get a visit from seagulls looking for the leftovers of your lunch. Many wading birds live on the coast, including curlews, plovers and sandpipers. They have long legs so that they can stand on the seabed and walk around looking for ragworms and crabs.

Razorbills

Mussels

Blue mussels are small creatures with shells that open like a locket. When the tide is out, the mussels keep their shells tightly closed. The shells are closed so tightly that even the strongest person in your class could not pull them apart. The shells are usually dark blue on the outside and silvery on the inside. Mussels are filter feeders. This means that they suck water into their bodies and spurt it back out. The mussel opens its shell and catches tiny creatures in a filter, or strainer, as the water passes through. Blue mussels can be eaten by humans.

Blue Mussel

Starfish

The starfish is not really a fish. It does not have gills, scales or fins. Scientists now call it a 'sea star'. Most sea stars have five arms, but some have 10 or more arms. They have no brains and no blood and can grow a new arm if one is bitten off by a bigger creature. Thousands of sea stars are sometimes washed onto the shore during storms. They die if they cannot get back to the sea. Sea stars love to eat mussels.

Starfish

Fish

Did you know that fish have cold blood? If they had warm blood, they would feel very cold in the Irish seawater. There are many types of fish close to the seashore. Fishermen catch mackerel, herring, flatfish, cod and many more. The body of a fish is covered in scales. Fins help the fish to swim through the water. Fish breathe through gills. Gills are openings that allow the fish to take oxygen from water.

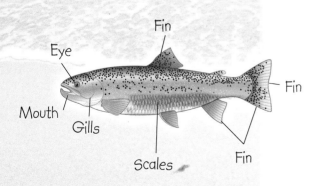

Fin
Eye
Fin
Mouth
Gills
Scales
Fin

| Subject: | Science | Strand: | Living Things |
| Strand Unit: | Plants and Animals | | |

| Subject: | Geography | Strand: | Natural Environments |
| Strand Unit: | The Local Natural Environment | | |

9

Ragworms and Lugworms

These worms live beneath the sand. You may have seen fishermen digging for them. They like to use them as bait. Birds like them too – for lunch, of course! Perhaps you have seen a squiggle of wet sand on the beach. Lugworms live beneath this mound in a tunnel in the shape of a U. They are about 15 centimetres long and can burrow through the sand very quickly. A ragworm has a red stripe on its back and it will give you a nasty bite if you pick it up. The ragworm can grow to a length of 30 centimetres.

Lugworm

Crabs

If you mention the word 'crabs' to a scientist, she will probably say, "Crabs... you mean decapods?" The word 'decapod' means '10 feet'. The crab uses eight of those to walk (sideways). The other two are sharp pincers. Do not get too close! Lobsters are also decapods. There are over 6000 types of crab in the world, including Hairy Crabs, Fiddler Crabs, Coconut Crabs and Hermit Crabs. Crabs are omnivores. They eat smaller sea creatures and almost anything else they can get their claws on. On an Irish seashore, you may come across Shore Crabs. They are usually brown in colour and their shells are about 6 centimetres wide. They need to stay wet, so you will find them in pools or sheltering under seaweed.

Crabs

Activities

1. How many legs has a crab?
2. What kind of mussel can be eaten by humans?
3. Write another name for the starfish.
4. Why is the starfish not really a fish?
5. Name a fish that you have eaten.
6. What does a fish's fin help it to do?
7. What does a fish use to breathe?
8. Name two types of worm that fishermen use as bait.
9. Are a wading bird's legs long or short?
10. Name as many fish as you can.

Subject:	Science	Strand:	Living Things	Subject:	Geography	Strand:	Natural Environments
Strand Unit:	Plants and Animals			Strand Unit:	The Local Natural Environment		

Jealous Wall,
Belvedere House

Buildings All Around Me

Just outside the town of Mullingar in County Westmeath, there is a beautiful old house called Belvedere House. It was built in 1740. The house belonged to a man called Robert Rochford, who was known as the 'Wicked Earl'. Robert did not like his brother, Arthur, and every time he looked out his window, he could see Arthur's house. The view of his brother's lovely house annoyed him, so he ordered that a high wall be built between the two houses. The wall is still there today and it is called the Jealous Wall.

When someone builds something with no real use, we call it a 'folly'. Most of the things that we build are useful. Look at the pictures below. Name each building.

Hot History

Robert had another interesting building. It was an ice house and was used to store food. There was no such thing as a fridge in 1740. The ice house was built underground and it was really cold. During the winter, ice was collected from the nearby lakes and stored in the ice house. The ice melted very slowly, but lasted well into summer.

| Subject: | Geography | Strand: | Human Environments |
| Strand Unit: | People Living and Working... (Homes and Other Buildings) |

| Subject: | Science | Strand: | Environmental Awareness and Care |
| Strand Unit: | Science and the Environment |

11

Homes in My Community

People live in different types of homes.

Terraced	Semi-detached	Detached
Bungalow	Apartment	Caravan

A house may have many different rooms. Most houses have a hall, stairs and landing, a kitchen, bathroom, living room, some bedrooms and perhaps, a dining room. Some houses may have a sunroom, walk-in wardrobe, attic, cellar, playroom or utility room with a washing machine and dryer. Some people work at home, so there might be an office, shop or farm buildings close by.

Activities

1. Think of a house that you know. It may be your own house or someone else's house.

   (a) Count the number of outside windows and doors.

   (b) Count the number of rooms in the house.

   (c) Write three sentences about the house. (For example, the house has a front garden and a back garden. The roof is…)

2. List 10 people who visit your home. (For example, Gran, bin collectors…)

3. To build a house, we need to use lots of materials. In which part of a house would you find each of the following materials?

concrete blocks	_walls_	paint	_____	tiles	_____
glass	_____	carpet	_____	curtains	_____
wood	_____	wires	_____	hinge	_____
slate	_____	pipes	_____	radiator	_____

Subject: Geography **Strand:** Human Environments
Strand Unit: People Living and Working… (Homes and Other Buildings)

Subject: Science **Strand:** Environmental Awareness and Care
Strand Unit: Science and the Environment

Cement and Concrete

Have you ever seen cement powder? It is grey in colour and it is really fine, like flour. It is so fine, that just 1 kilogramme has more than 300 billion tiny grains of cement! You could easily get it through a sieve. When cement is mixed with water, it sets after a few hours and becomes as hard as rock. Builders mix cement with water and sand to make concrete. You have probably seen concrete blocks being used to build walls and houses.

Concrete

Cement powder

Cement mixer

What Is in a House?

People usually live in houses. A house needs two important things: water and power. We use water for drinking, cooking, washing, ironing, heating, brushing our teeth and flushing the toilet. Water comes to our homes through underground pipes, all the way from a lake or reservoir. A reservoir is a natural or man-made

Vartry Reservoir, County Wicklow

lake, where water is kept or stored. A man-made reservoir is usually made from concrete. Many houseowners now have to pay for their water. The more water they use, the more they pay. It is not sensible to waste water. Many homes have both electricity and gas. These also have to be paid for. It is definitely not a good idea to waste electricity.

What are Solar Panels?

Solar panel on a roof

Solar panels can be used to heat water in a house. They are built into the roof. Usually they are on the side that faces south, so that they always face the sun. Solar panels spend the day sunbathing! They collect energy from the sun and use that energy to heat water. They work all year round, but they work best in the summer months.

| Subject: | Geography | Strand: | Human Environments |
| Strand Unit: | People Living and Working... (Homes and Other Buildings) | | |

| Subject: | Science | Strand: | Environmental Awareness and Care |
| Strand Unit: | Science and the Environment | | |

13

Bridges

How did people cross a river in the past if there was no bridge? They had to find a shallow part of the river and get their feet wet! The crossing places were called fords. All those wet feet made people think about building bridges across rivers. Bridges are very difficult to build. They have to be strong enough to carry people, animals and lorries. They need to be tall enough to allow boats to pass underneath. They have to be strong enough that they will not be swept away if the river floods.

Hot History

You may have read about the 'Fight at the Ford', one of Ireland's most famous legends. The legend tells us how Cúchulainn killed his best friend, Ferdia, after a fight that lasted three days.

What Is an Arch?

Keystone

The Ancient Romans invented the arch. It is a very strong type of building that is perfect for bridges. If the arch is high enough, boats that are very tall can pass underneath. Bridges with arches were built over the River Shannon, the River Lee, the River Liffey and many other rivers in Ireland. The arches are still standing today. To make an arch, the builders use bricks in the shape of wedges. The bricks curve around, as shown in the picture. At the top, a special brick is put in place. This is called the keystone.

Types of Bridge

Arch bridge	Drawbridge	Beam bridge	Cable stay bridge
The most famous arch bridge in the world is the Sydney Harbour Bridge in Australia.	This type of bridge has a deck that can be pulled aside or pulled up to allow boats to pass. Tower Bridge in London is a drawbridge.	Beam bridges have been around for thousands of years. Pillars are planted in the ground and the bridge is built on top. The Bang Na Bridge in Thailand is 55 kilometres long!	Steel cables connect the bridge to giant pillars. The William Dargan Bridge for the Luas in Dundrum in Dublin is a cable stay bridge.

Subject: Geography **Strand:** Human Environments
Strand Unit: People Living and Working... (Homes and Other Buildings)

Subject: Science **Strand:** Environmental Awareness and Care
Strand Unit: Science and the Environment

Without a Home

Imagine life without a home. People who have no place to live are homeless. Their lives can be very hard, especially in the wintertime. Sometimes they sleep in parks or under bridges – any place that gives them some shelter. They have no place to wash or cook or feel safe. They have nowhere to leave the things that they own, so they have to carry everything with them. Members of your community help homeless people by running soup kitchens. Late at night, flasks of soup and sandwiches are brought to places where homeless people gather. That food might be the only thing that they have eaten that day.

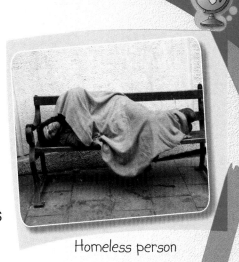

Homeless person

Activities

A. Write Each of the Following.

1. Four types of house. (For example, terraced.)
2. Four rooms in a house.
3. Four things that are made from concrete.
4. Four things that might come to your house through a pipe or wire.

B. Answer the Questions.

1. What is a ford in a river?
2. What is an arch?
3. Which ancient people invented the arch?
4. Where in an arch is the keystone?
5. Name four types of bridge.

C. What Would You Expect to Find in Each Building? Match the Pairs.

Set 1		Set 2	
hospital	• pupil	court	• meals
bank	• doctor	restaurant	• books
school	• king	warehouse	• judge
palace	• tomatoes	library	• old things
greenhouse	• money	museum	• boxes

Subject: Geography   **Strand:** Human Environments
Strand Unit: People Living and Working... (Homes and Other Buildings)

Subject: Science   **Strand:** Environmental Awareness and Care
Strand Unit: Science and the Environment

15

Fruit and Vegetables

Raspberries

Raspberries are red fruits that grow in summer on the branches of a bush. Raspberries contain lots of vitamin C and fibre and they make delicious jam.

Raspberries

Strawberries

Strawberries grow with their seeds on the outside. The strawberry plant is a member of the rose family. Lots of strawberries are grown in County Wexford.

Strawberries

Blackberries

Blackberries grow wild on the sides of roads and can be picked in September.

Blackcurrants

Blackcurrants are richer in vitamin C than oranges. The juice of this fruit is very good for soothing sore throats.

Blackberries

Tomatoes

The tomato is a fruit, but do not try putting it in a fruit salad! In Ireland, tomatoes grow best in greenhouses, because they like heat and light.

Blackcurrants

Cabbages

Cabbage contains lots of water and it is one of the oldest vegetables known to humans. It is a very healthy vegetable and it is also used to make coleslaw.

Tomatoes

Cabbages

Broccoli

Broccoli

This vegetable is the young flower, or bud, of the broccoli plant. It is full of vitamins.

Onions

Onions are the most popular vegetables in the world for flavouring. When an onion is cut, acids are released. The acids can make you cry when they reach your eyes!

Onions

Carrots

Carrots are good for your eyesight – have you ever seen a rabbit wearing glasses? In the past, European carrots were purple. Dutch farmers discovered orange carrots and they started to grow them in honour of their hero, whose name was William of Orange!

Carrots

Beetroot

Beetroot contains more sugar than most vegetables. This 'good' sugar is released slowly into the body. People once used beetroot juice to dye their hair!

Beetroot

Potatoes

Potatoes are the fourth most important crop in the world (after wheat, corn and rice). The potato was the first vegetable grown in outer space, aboard a spaceship. Potatoes are a very healthy vegetable.

Parsnip

Long ago, parsnips were added to jams and cakes to make them sweet. In Italy, pigs that are bred for their famous Parma ham are often fed parsnips.

Potatoes

Parsnips

Unit 3: Plants and Habitats

New Words

| meadow | oxygen | marram grass | fertilise |

HERE ARE SOME SEEDS FOR YOU TO PLANT.

I THINK THE WEATHER IS TOO COLD.

I THINK WE COULD PLANT THEM INDOORS.

I THINK IT DEPENDS ON THE TYPE OF SEED.

The Fox and the Bear

The fox and the bear decided to set up a business.

"We must be fair," said Bear.

"Oh yes," replied Fox, "we'll split everything 50-50. Let's grow some wheat. I'll take everything that grows above the ground and you'll take everything that grows under the ground."

That sounded fair to Bear, but of course when the wheat was ripe, only the seeds (which grow above the ground) were any good. Poor Bear got nothing.

The following year, crafty Fox asked Bear if he would like to do business again.

"Yes I would," said Bear, "but this year, I'll get everything that grows above the ground."

"Fair enough," said Fox, "I think we'll grow carrots this year."

Planting Seeds

Many plants grow from seeds. We usually plant vegetable and flower seeds in spring. They grow and get bigger during summer and give us beautiful flowers and tasty vegetables. Seeds are very choosy about where they grow! They do not grow just anywhere. Seeds and plants need four important things to grow: heat, water, light and good soil.

Heat

Seeds and plants do not like cold weather. Think of a garden in winter: many of the plants have died and others are asleep, waiting for the weather to get warmer.

ZZZzzzzz

Water

If you plant seeds and forget to water them, they will not grow. They will not even start to grow! They will stay asleep, waiting for rain or water from a watering can.

Light

Plants love light. If you plant seeds in a cupboard that is warm and dark, the seeds will pop up looking for light. However, they will soon die if they are left in the dark.

Good Soil

Seeds and plants grow best in soil that has not too many stones, has plenty of air, is not too damp, is not too dry, is warm and has plenty of earthworms. Some seeds like to be planted on the soil; some prefer to be planted in the soil, but not too deeply. Others like to have lots of soil on top of them before they will even think about growing. Seeds are choosy!

| Subject: | Science | Strand: | Living Things |
| Strand Unit: | Plants and Animals |

| Subject: | Geography | Strand: | Natural Environments |
| Strand Unit: | The Local Natural Environment |

Plants Make Food

Plants grow below the ground as well as above the ground. The part of the plant that grows below the ground is called the root. It gathers water and food from the soil. Plants carry out two very important jobs for us. Firstly, they help to fill the air that we breathe with oxygen. Oxygen is a gas that we cannot see, but we need it to live. Secondly, with the help of sunlight, plants make food, which we can eat.

I THINK THAT IF THERE WERE NO PLANTS IN THE WORLD, THERE WOULD BE NO ANIMALS EITHER.

Potatoes	Strawberries	Wheat
Potatoes came to Ireland from America over 400 years ago. Potatoes grow under the ground. In Ireland, we plant potatoes outdoors after Saint Patrick's Day and they are ready to harvest in August.	Strawberries are a delicious, red fruit. They are ripe in June and July. County Wexford is famous for strawberries, because it is in the sunny South-east of Ireland.	Wheat is a type of grass. Its seeds are collected and ground into flour. Bread and pasta are made from wheat. Wheat is grown in Ireland, but it grows best in countries where there is lots of sunshine in the summer.

Activities

A. Fill in the Blanks.

Plants need _____, _____ and _____ in order to grow. They grow best when they are planted in good _____. Part of the plant grows _____ the ground and part of it grows _____ the ground. Humans like to eat plants. We eat _____ (such as apples and strawberries) and _____ (such as carrots and parsnips). Plants fill our air with _____.

B. Make a Fact File.

Much of the food that we eat began life as, or on, a plant. Chocolate, for example, started life as a cocoa bean. We eat other things that are not plants: fish, for example. Draw two boxes called 'Plants we eat' and 'Other foods.' Write 10 items in each.

Meadow

Fields and Meadows

Meadows are full of living things such as grass, daisies, dandelions, clover, buttercups, shamrock, mushrooms, insects, butterflies, worms, snails, rabbits and much more. Visitors to Ireland from warmer countries are often amazed at how green our country looks. Ireland is sometimes called the Emerald Isle. (An emerald is a precious, green stone.)

Grass

Think of the many places where grass grows: farms, gardens, football pitches, golf courses, etc. Grass is nice to look at and nice to eat (if you are a cow or sheep!). There are thousands of types of grass. The grass family is the most important food-plant family in the world. Wheat, barley and sugarcane are types of grass. Some grass, such as pampas grass, can grow taller than a human!

Daisy and Dandelion

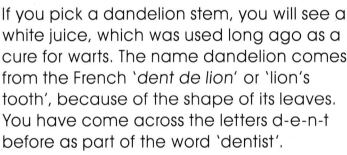
Daisy

Look closely at a daisy and you will see an eye. This is where the name daisy comes from: 'day's eye'. It even closes at night, just like you do when you fall asleep. Daisies live from year to year. You do not need to plant daisy seeds. Have you ever made a daisy chain?

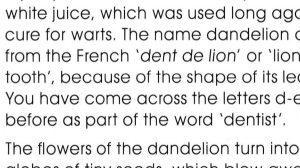
Dandelion

If you pick a dandelion stem, you will see a white juice, which was used long ago as a cure for warts. The name dandelion comes from the French 'dent de lion' or 'lion's tooth', because of the shape of its leaves. You have come across the letters d-e-n-t before as part of the word 'dentist'.

Jinny-joe

The flowers of the dandelion turn into globes of tiny seeds, which blow away on a breezy summer's day. Have you ever picked a jinny-joe and blown the seeds away?

White Clover and Shamrock

White clover

White clover and shamrock each have three leaves. Shamrock is smaller than clover and Irish people all over the world wear it on Saint Patrick's Day.

Hot History

It is said that it is lucky to find a four-leaf clover. The first leaf brings faith, the second brings hope, the third brings love and the fourth is for luck!

Subject:	Science	Strand:	Living Things
Strand Unit:	Plants and Animals		

Subject:	Geography	Strand:	Natural Environments
Strand Unit:	The Local Natural Environment		

Seashore

The Seashore

Have you ever walked along a sandy beach? The plants you see are very different from those that grow in a meadow or field. The tide comes in and goes out twice every day. It takes the tide about $6\frac{1}{4}$ hours to come in and about $6\frac{1}{4}$ hours to go out. Plants living on the seashore have to put up with wind, water and salt. The seashore is not the easiest place to live. Let's look at some plants that live there.

Spring tides happen twice a month: when the moon is full and when the moon is new. Spring tides are high tides and they happen in every season. The word 'spring' comes from the old word 'springen', which means 'jump'.

Sea Pinks

Plants that live near the top of the shore, away from the water, need to be very tough. They are lashed by the wind and sprayed by the salty sea. Seapinks look like meadow plants, but their leaves are rough and narrow.

Sea pinks

Marram Grass

This type of grass lives in sand dunes, where the sand is often dry and fine and easily blown away by the wind. Imagine trying to eat and drink if someone kept moving your plate and cup! Marram grass has roots that are really long and strong. The roots help to stop the sand from blowing away. Marram grass has been planted in many places around Ireland to stop the beach from disappearing.

Marram grass

Seaweed

Green seaweed

Most seaweed is green, brown or red. Seaweed that floats or lives on the shore is green. Seaweed that lives mostly underwater is brown or red. Seaweed has many uses. It has lots of minerals and vitamins, which help to keep us healthy. Some people collect it and use it to fertilise their fields and gardens. Many people eat it and others bathe in special seaweed baths!

Things to Look Out for On the Seashore

Beaches that are very clean are given a special blue flag. Ireland has many beaches with blue flags. Another type of flag you might see on the beach is the lifeguard's flag. This is yellow and red and tells us that the lifeguard is on duty. A red flag means that it is not safe to swim.

Blue flag (clean beach)

Danger (not safe to swim)

Lifeguard's flag (on duty)

Subject:	Science	Strand:	Living Things
Strand Unit:	Plants and Animals		

Subject:	Geography	Strand:	Natural Environments
Strand Unit:	The Local Natural Environment		

Seeds

Some seeds can live for a long time before springing into life. Seeds have been found frozen in the ground after thousands of years and when they thawed out, they grew. Humans love to eat seeds. When you eat breakfast cereal, bread or pasta, you are eating food made from seeds! Some seeds are highly poisonous. The kidney bean is a seed that can kill if it is not soaked and cooked properly.

The coconut is the largest seed in the world and it floats! Coconuts can float for hundreds of kilometres before finding a good place to grow.

Investigate: What Do Seeds Need to Grow?

You will need: Four pots, bean or pea seeds, compost, water, watering can
Method: Find out if seeds will grow without water, light or soil.

1. Label the pots: 'A control', 'B no water', 'C no light' and 'D no soil'.
2. Fill pots A, B and C with compost.
3. Put three seeds in each pot.
4. Water all of the pots except pot B.
5. Place all of the pots somewhere warm and bright.
6. Put a paper bag over pot C.
7. Record the results on the record sheet in your Activity Book.

Activities

A. Find the Mistake in Each Sentence. Write the Sentence Correctly.

1. It is dangerous to swim if you see a blue flag.
2. Marram grass stops sand from drying out.
3. Good soil has no earthworms.
4. Potatoes went from Ireland to America.
5. Spring tides only happen in spring.

B. Answer the Following Questions.

1. What type of plant is wheat?
2. What plant's name comes from 'day's eye'?
3. Nettles are found in many fields. What happens if you touch a nettle?
4. Name a plant that adds flavour to food.
5. How many animals that graze in fields and meadows can you think of? List them.
6. Imagine that you are sitting in a meadow on a nice sunny day. Can you think of 10 sounds that you might hear?

| Subject: | Science | Strand: | Living Things | Subject: | Geography | Strand: | Natural Environments |
| Strand Unit: | Plants and Animals | | | Strand Unit: | The Local Natural Environment | | |

New Words

| application | median | council | colony |

Cast Away

The year was 2004 and Thomas Leaf (known to his pals as 'Tealeaf') was sailing his small boat off the north coast of Australia. Suddenly the wind rose and Tealeaf decided to return to the shore. However, the wind changed direction and his boat was carried far out to sea. Tealeaf was barely able to cling on. By the time the storm had ended, the coast of Australia was out of sight. Tealeaf was washed ashore on a small island. No one lived on the island. There were plenty of trees and birds and Tealeaf was delighted to find a stream with fresh water. His mobile phone did not work and he had to wait for someone to rescue him. It was nearly two weeks before he was found.

Shipwreck Survivor Speaks to Reporter

Reporter: You had a lucky escape. How do you feel?

Tealeaf: Very hungry. Very tired.

Reporter: What did you eat while you were on the island?

Tealeaf: I found a few crabs and some coconuts. I had no way of making a fire, so I had to eat the crabmeat raw – not so nice.

Reporter: Was there any shelter on the island?

Tealeaf: Just some trees to shade me from the hot sun, but it was very cold during the night. I was only wearing light clothes.

Reporter: Were you scared?

Tealeaf: Really scared. My mobile phone wouldn't work and I was afraid that people might give up searching for me.

Reporter: It must have been strange being by yourself.

Tealeaf: Sure was, mate. No shops, no electricity, no TV, no car, no friends.

Reporter: Tell us what you missed the most.

Tealeaf: I missed people. There was no one to talk to, no one to get help from. I never realised how much I depend on other people.

Being cast away on an island may sound great, but in fact, it is very difficult. You would have to do everything for yourself and you would have no one to complain to!

| **Subject:** Geography | **Strand:** Human Environments |
| **Strand Unit:** People Living and Working... (Communities) |

| **Subject:** Science | **Strand:** Environmental Awareness and Care |
| **Strand Unit:** Caring for the Environment |

23

We Depend on Each Other

Megan is nine years old. The diagram below shows
some of the people on whom Megan depends.

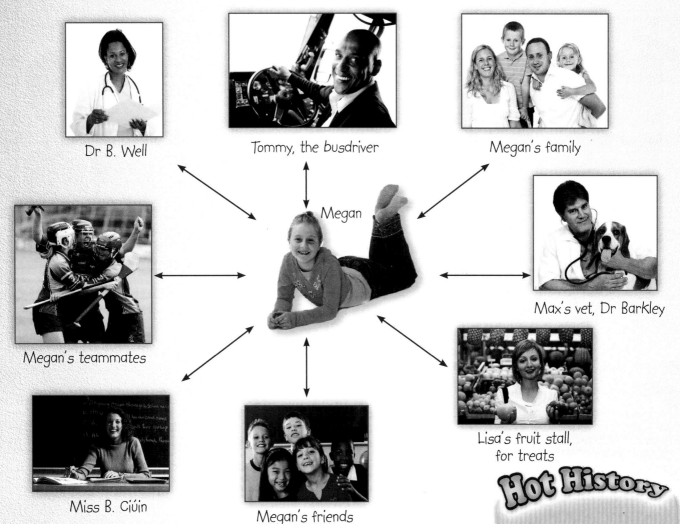

Dr B. Well

Tommy, the busdriver

Megan's family

Megan

Max's vet, Dr Barkley

Megan's teammates

Lisa's fruit stall,
for treats

Miss B. Ciúin

Megan's friends

There are many other people on whom Megan depends
and there are lots of people who depend on Megan.
Megan lives in a community. A community is a group
of people who live or work near each other and help
each other out. Your classmates and schoolmates are a
community. Your teacher helps you to learn to read and
write. You help your classmates and they help you.

Hot History

Long ago, children
were sometimes taught
in their homes by a
tutor or a governess.
Do you think that would
be a good way to learn
your lessons? What
about friends?

Activities

1. What do you think you would miss most if you were cast away? Make a list of 10 things.

2. If you knew you were going to be cast away and you could bring five books with you,
   which five would you choose?

3. Draw a diagram like Megan's, showing some of the people on whom you depend.

| Subject: | Geography | Strand: | Human Environments |
| Strand Unit: | People Living and Working... (Communities) |

| Subject: | Science | Strand: | Environmental Awareness and Care |
| Strand Unit: | Caring for the Environment |

A Look at Your Community

The people who live and work in the houses and shops around you all form a community. There are clubs and groups, where people with the same interests come together: swimming clubs, camera clubs and sports clubs.

Megan thought she might like to join a local science club. Look at the application form that Megan filled out. If you join a club, always ask an adult to help you with the application form. Remember to tell your family everything that happened while you were there.

Community to the Rescue

Mrs Kelly is Megan's neighbour. Last Tuesday, Mrs Kelly opened her front door and Sparky, her dog, ran out. She called him, but he ran off down the road.

"Never mind," she thought. "He'll come back when he's hungry."

Name:	Megan Sweet
Address:	21, The Elms, Grange
Email:	megans@sciencemail.ie
Age:	9
Interests:	Experiments, plants and animals

Tick the box that best describes you:

Fun and friendly ☐
Sporty and cheerful ☐
Serious and kind ☑

Why do you wish to join our science club?
To learn about science (which I really love) and to make new friends

Parent's Signature: *J. M. Sweet*

The club meets in the hall on Fridays at 4 pm.
Bring an apron and gloves.
Joining Fee: €2.50
Note to new members: Professor P. Nutts will be visiting on the 25th. Make sure you're on time!

That afternoon, Megan's dad was driving along the main street on his way to collect Megan from school. Suddenly he spotted Sparky. He was sitting on the median in the middle of the road, looking very scared. The road was very busy

and if Sparky moved, he would be sure to cause an accident. Dad had an idea. He knew that the school warden would be finished work in a few minutes' time. He parked his car, collected Megan and asked Helen, the warden, if she could help. Helen was happy to help. She walked up the street with Dad and Megan, carrying her STOP sign. She stopped the traffic and Dad rescued Sparky. Dad and Megan brought Sparky back safely to Mrs Kelly.

Subject:	Geography	Strand:	Human Environments
Strand Unit:	People Living and Working... (Communities)		

Subject:	Science	Strand:	Environmental Awareness and Care
Strand Unit:	Caring for the Environment		

25

What is the Council?

Friends and neighbours in your community will help you when they can. However, here are some things they may not be able to do:

- Run a library
- Empty recycling bins
- Collect stray dogs and horses
- Clean the streets
- Look after parks and football fields
- Fix the roads

Many of those jobs are done by the council. Every county has a council. The council office is probably in the main town in your county. Every day, the council workers try to make your community a nicer place in which to live. Noel works for the council. Let's look at the work that he does.

Hi, my name is Noel and I work for the council. Here are some of the jobs that I did last week:

Monday: I spent the day working in Leafy Park. People had lit a bonfire during the weekend and I had to clean up the mess.

Tuesday: I worked for the road crew. We had to fix some potholes on the R2521.

Wednesday: I got a call from a school. The hurling team wanted to play a match in the park. I had to cut the grass and put up the nets.

Thursday: My favourite day – pay day! I unblocked the pipes in the swimming pool.

Friday: I emptied the recycling bins in all of the shopping centres. We do this on Friday because lots of people visit the bottle banks at the weekend.

Others in Your Community

Your community has lots of people with skills or talents. Someone teaches the guitar; another person is a great baker; someone else visits elderly people. Each person makes your community a better place. Your community has police officers and fire officers. If you live near the sea, there may be a coastguard service. Those people make your community a safer place in which to live. It is up to everyone to play their part in the community. Helping each other out makes your street, town or village a nicer place.

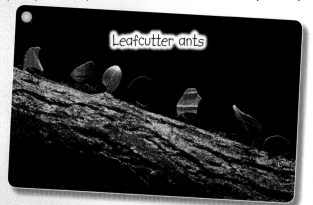

Leafcutter ants

Animals and Communities

Some creatures like to live and work alone, but many animals live in communities. Honeybees work in a hive. Wolves hunt in packs. Dolphins swim in schools (no, not your kind of school!). Ants work in a colony. Each ant works for the good of the whole community and not just for itself.

Subject:	Geography	Strand:	Human Environments
Strand Unit:	People Living and Working... (Communities)		

Subject:	Science	Strand:	Environmental Awareness and Care
Strand Unit:	Caring for the Environment		

Activities

A. Design a Form.

Look at Megan's application form on page 25. Design and fill in a form like Megan's for the local reading club. Include lots of sensible questions such as:
What book are you reading at the moment? Name a book that you really enjoyed.

B. Write the Answers.

Megan carried out a survey about litter in her community. She met two people and asked the following questions. What do you think they said?

Mrs Ryan	Mr Poole
Megan: Hi there, do you mind if I ask you a few questions? Mrs Ryan: _____	Megan: Hi there, do you mind if I ask you a few questions? Mr Poole: _____
Megan: What kind of litter have you seen on your street? Mrs Ryan: _____	Megan: What kind of litter have you seen on your street? Mr Poole: _____
Megan: Do you think there are enough litter bins around? Mrs Ryan: _____	Megan: Do you think there are enough litter bins around? Mr Poole: _____
Megan: What could we do to make our community a cleaner place in which to live? Mrs Ryan: _____	Megan: What could we do to make our community a cleaner place in which to live? Mr Poole: _____
Megan: We are planning a litter clean-up on Saturday morning. Do you think you'd be able to help for an hour? Mrs Ryan: _____	Megan: We are planning a litter clean-up on Saturday morning. Do you think you'd be able to help for an hour? Mr Poole: _____
Megan: Okay, thanks for your time.	Megan: Okay, thanks for your time.

C. Digging Deeper.

Read Aesop's Fable, *The Ant and the Grasshopper*.

Political Map of Ireland

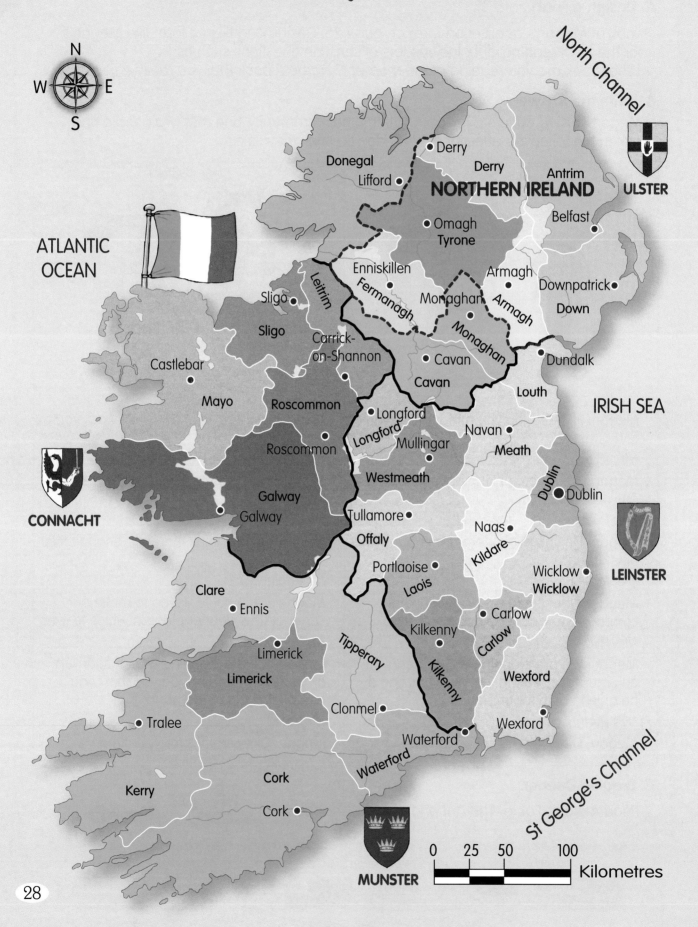

North Channel

N
W E
S

ATLANTIC
OCEAN

ULSTER

Donegal
Lifford
Derry
Derry
Antrim
NORTHERN IRELAND
Belfast
Omagh
Tyrone
Enniskillen
Fermanagh
Armagh
Downpatrick
Monaghan
Armagh
Down
Sligo
Leitrim
Monaghan
Sligo
Carrick-on-Shannon
Cavan
Dundalk
Castlebar
Cavan
Louth
Mayo
Roscommon
Longford
Longford
Navan
IRISH SEA
Roscommon
Mullingar
Meath
Westmeath
Dublin
Galway
Dublin
Galway
Tullamore
Naas
Offaly
Kildare
Portlaoise
Wicklow
Clare
Laois
Wicklow
Ennis
Carlow
Limerick
Kilkenny
Carlow
Tipperary
Limerick
Kilkenny
Wexford
Tralee
Clonmel
Wexford
Waterford
Kerry
Waterford
Cork
Cork

CONNACHT

LEINSTER

MUNSTER

St George's Channel

0 25 50   100
Kilometres

Physical Map of Ireland

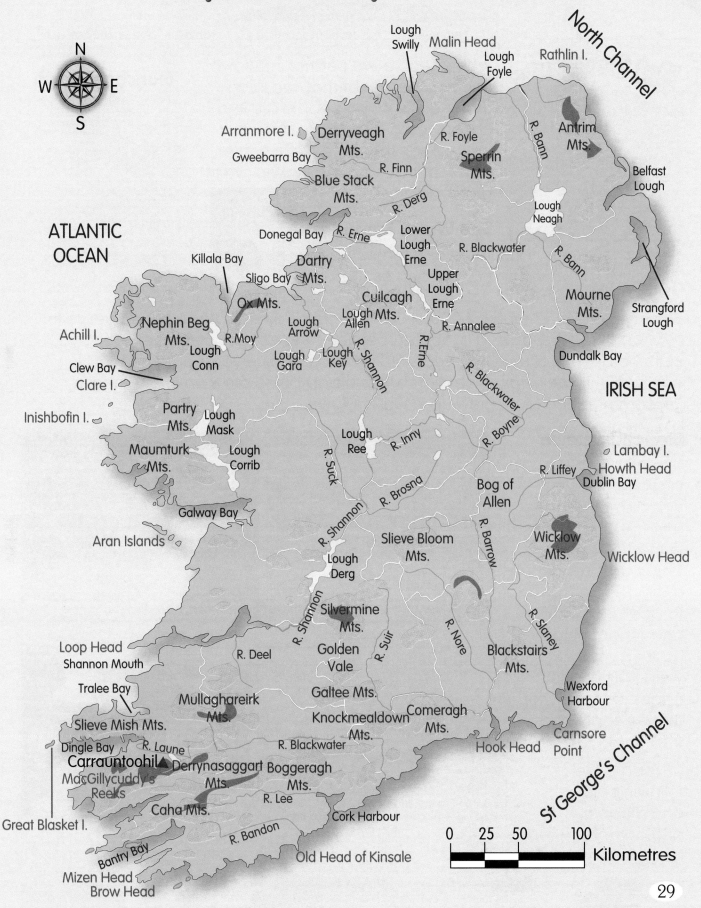

N
W E
S

North Channel

Lough Swilly
Malin Head
Lough Foyle
Rathlin I.

Arranmore I.
Derryveagh Mts.
R. Foyle
Antrim Mts.

Gweebarra Bay
R. Finn
Sperrin Mts.
R. Bann
Belfast Lough

ATLANTIC OCEAN

Blue Stack Mts.
R. Derg
Lough Neagh

Killala Bay
Donegal Bay
R. Erne
Lower Lough Erne
R. Blackwater
R. Bann

Sligo Bay
Dartry Mts.
Upper Lough Erne
Mourne Mts.

Ox Mts.
Cuilcagh Mts.
R. Annalee
Strangford Lough

Nephin Beg Mts.
Lough Arrow
Lough Allen

Achill I.
R. Moy
Lough Conn
Lough Gara
Lough Key
R. Shannon
R. Blackwater
Dundalk Bay

Clew Bay
Clare I.
R. Erne
IRISH SEA

Inishbofin I.
Partry Mts.
Lough Mask
Lough Ree
R. Inny
R. Boyne
Lambay I.
Howth Head

Maumturk Mts.
Lough Corrib
R. Suck
R. Brosna
Bog of Allen
R. Liffey
Dublin Bay

Galway Bay

Aran Islands
Slieve Bloom Mts.
R. Barrow
Wicklow Mts.
Wicklow Head

Lough Derg

R. Shannon

Loop Head
R. Deel
Silvermine Mts.
R. Suir
R. Nore
Blackstairs Mts.
R. Slaney

Shannon Mouth
Golden Vale

Tralee Bay
Mullaghareirk Mts.
Galtee Mts.
Comeragh Mts.
Wexford Harbour

Slieve Mish Mts.
Knockmealdown Mts.
Carnsore Point

Dingle Bay
R. Laune
R. Blackwater
Hook Head

Carrauntoohil
Derrynasaggart Mts.
Boggeragh Mts.

MacGillycuddy's Reeks
R. Lee

Great Blasket I.
Caha Mts.
R. Bandon
Cork Harbour

Bantry Bay
Old Head of Kinsale

Mizen Head
Brow Head

St George's Channel

0   25   50   100

Kilometres

Unit 5: Life in Blanchardstown

New Words

urban   rural   suburb   commute   residents' association   graffiti   emergency services

Hot Geography

A suburb is an area with lots of houses on the edge of a large city or town. People who work in a city or town often live in a suburb and commute (travel) to work.

When people live near or in a town or city, we say that they live in an urban area. When people live in a country area away from a town or city, we say that they live in a rural area. Let's meet a family who live in an urban area.

The Walsh Family

The Walsh family lives in a housing estate called Luttrell Way in

The Walshs

Blanchardstown

- County: Dublin
- Province: Leinster
- Population: 68,000

Blanchardstown, a suburb of Dublin City. Luttrell Way is a large housing estate in the north-west of Dublin. It is located between the villages of Castleknock and Blanchardstown. Niamh is 15 years old and Jack is nine years old. The family has lived in Luttrell Way since Niamh was a baby. Dad grew up in a village in Roscommon and Mum grew up in Cavan Town.

Blanchardstown

Up until the 1960s, Blanchardstown was a small village surrounded by fields. In the 1970s and 1980s, more and more people moved to Dublin for work and school. Huge housing estates were built on the edges of the city for those people and their families.

Compare the following old and modern photographs to see how the area has changed.

Aerial view of Blanchardstown, 1950s

Google Earth of Blanchardstown, 2012

Main Street Blanchardstown, 1900s

Main Street Blanchardstown, 2012

30

Subject: Geography   Strand: Human Environments
Strand Unit: People Living and Working in a Contrasting Part of Ireland

Subject: Science   Strand: Environmental Awareness and Care
Strand Unit: Environmental Awareness

The Walshs' Community

There are now more than 68,000 people living in Blanchardstown, including people from many countries around the world. The Walsh family have friends and neighbours from Poland, Lithuania, Bosnia and Pakistan. The Walshs live in a three-bedroom, semi-detached house. There are hundreds of similar houses in the estate. Three years ago, they turned the attic into a guest bedroom and play area. They have no garage, so the car is parked in the driveway. They keep the children's bicycles in a wooden shed in the small back garden.

The Walshs' house

Collecting litter

A residents' association has been set up in the estate. They have a clean-up twice a year. The children join in and pick up litter in the streets and green areas. The adults cut back the shrubs and clean up any graffiti on the walls and lanes.

Most of the houses in the Walshs' estate have burglar alarms. During Community Safety Week, the Walsh family visited the Garda Station in Blanchardstown and learned all about the important work of the local emergency services.

Blanchardstown Garda Station

Hot Geography

Many hedgerows in the suburbs of Blanchardstown were cut down to make way for houses. The hedgerows that still grow along the railway line and the Royal Canal are protected by law.

The Walshs' Friends

Across the road from the Walshs' house, there is a small row of new terraced houses. Their friends, the O'Donnells, live there. There are no spaces between the houses. At the front of each house there is a small flowerbed and just enough space to park a car. The O'Donnells have built a wooden deck at the back of the house and they invite the Walshs over for barbeques during the summer months.

The O'Donnells' street

The Walshs' friends from Bosnia, the Terzić family, live in a second-floor apartment close to Blanchardstown Village. They have two bedrooms, a kitchen/living area and a bathroom. They have a small balcony, where they keep potted plants. There is also a shared garden at the back of the apartment block.

The Terzićs' apartment block

Subject:	Geography	Strand:	Human Environments
Strand Unit:	People Living and Working in a Contrasting Part of Ireland		

Subject:	Science	Strand:	Environmental Awareness and Care
Strand Unit:	Environmental Awareness		

Activities

A. Choose the Correct Answer to Complete Each Sentence.

1. A suburb is *an area with lots of houses on the edge of a large town*

   (a) a village in the countryside,

   (b) the centre of a city, where there are lots of shops, or

   (c) an area with lots of houses on the edge of a large town or city

2. Blanchardstown is a suburb of _____.

   (a) Galway, **(b)** Dublin, or **(c)** Athlone

3. The O'Donnell family live in a _____ house.

   (a) detached, **(b)** terraced, or **(c)** semi-detached

4. Blanchardstown has a population of around _____.

   (a) 600, **(b)** 6800, or **(c)** 68,000

5. The Walsh family live in a _____ house.

   (a) detached, **(b)** semi-detached, or **(c)** terraced

B. Think About It.

1. Write each of the following words and phrases in sentences.

   (a) residents' association, **(b)** apartment, **(c)** urban, **(d)** rural, **(e)** commute, **(f)** graffiti, **(g)** terraced house

2. Make a list of the good and bad things about living in a city.

Hot Geography

Cycling is good for you. Cycling to work and school means that cities have less pollution and fewer traffic jams. Dublin has a public bicycle scheme. You can borrow a bicycle and return it at another location for a small fee.

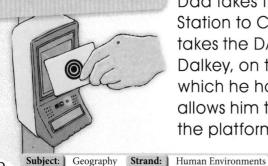

How Mum and Dad Commute to Work

Many people moved to Blanchardstown from all over Ireland and abroad to get work. Some people work in the Blanchardstown area, but many work in the city centre. Mum's office is in the city centre. When the weather is good, she likes to cycle to work. There are safe cycle lanes on the sides of the road. When the weather is bad, Mum usually takes the number 37 bus into the city centre. There are lots of buses at peak times, when people are travelling to and from work. Because of the traffic, it takes almost an hour for the bus to reach the city centre.

Dad takes the Maynooth Suburban Train from Coolmine Station to Connolly Station in the city centre. Then he takes the DART from Connolly Station to his office in Dalkey, on the south side of Dublin. He has a Leap Card, which he holds up to a sensor machine in each station. It allows him to walk through an electronic gate and onto the platform without having to buy a ticket each day.

Subject:	Geography	Strand:	Human Environments
Strand Unit:	People Living and Working in a Contrasting Part of Ireland		

Subject:	Science	Strand:	Environmental Awareness and Care
Strand Unit:	Environmental Awareness		

Niamh and Jack's Schools

Niamh and Jack can walk to their local schools. There are 10 primary schools and several secondary schools within easy reach of their home. Niamh is old enough to walk home for lunch every day. Jack is collected by minibus when his school finishes at 2:30 pm. He is dropped at the local crèche, where he eats his dinner, does his homework and plays with his friends until Mum or Dad collect him at 6:00 pm. In a few years' time, Niamh hopes to go to college. The Institute of Technology, Blanchardstown is very close to the Walshs' house. The National University of Ireland, Maynooth is only a 20-minute train journey away.

National University of Ireland, Maynooth

Weekends

The Walshs go to a local shop around the corner when they need a small number of items. They do their weekly shopping at the supermarket in Blanchardstown Village. On Saturdays, the family goes to the Blanchardstown Centre. This is a huge shopping centre, where people from all over Ireland come to shop – especially

Blanchardstown Centre

in the busy times before Christmas. Niamh goes to the Centre with her friends on Saturdays. They walk around the shops, get something to eat and go to the cinema. Jack likes the bowling alley at the Leisureplex in the Centre.

Leisure Activities

Niamh is a member of a local swimming club. She trains every evening in the National Aquatic Centre in Blanchardstown. It has an

National Aquatic Centre

Olympic-size swimming pool. Mum goes to yoga classes in the local community centre a few times a week to keep fit. Dad likes to take the dog for a walk in one of the nearby parks. Many of the parks within walking distance have playgrounds and football pitches, where Jack likes to play with his friends. There is a skate-park and a huge playground in the local Millennium Park in Blanchardstown. On weekends, the family often goes to the Phoenix Park.

Hot Geography

Áras an Uachtaráin, in the Phoenix Park, is the home of the President of Ireland.

Áras an Uachtaráin

Almost one-third of the park is covered in native trees. The park is home to a herd of fallow deer. Dublin Zoo is one of the greatest attractions for visitors to the park.

| Subject: | Geography | Strand: | Human Environments |
| Strand Unit: | People Living and Working in a Contrasting Part of Ireland |

| Subject: | Science | Strand: | Environmental Awareness and Care |
| Strand Unit: | Environmental Awareness |

33

Buildings of Interest in the Locality

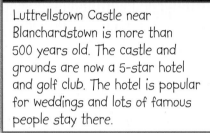
Luttrellstown Castle near Blanchardstown is more than 500 years old. The castle and grounds are now a 5-star hotel and golf club. The hotel is popular for weddings and lots of famous people stay there.

This photograph shows a high-rise block of offices in Blanchardstown. Many local people are employed in the offices of big companies such as IBM, eBay and Xerox.

Connolly Memorial Hospital has a very busy emergency department. Many of the doctors and nurses who work in the hospital live in the Blanchardstown area.

Activities

A. Answer the Questions.

1. Which bus does Mum take from Blanchardstown to the city centre?
2. What is the name of the local train station in Blanchardstown?
3. What is the name of the big shopping centre in Blanchardstown?
4. Name a leisure park near the Walshs' home.
5. List three things that you might see in the Phoenix Park.
6. Where does Niamh swim?
7. What is the name of the castle in the area?
8. What is the name of the local hospital?

B. Think About It.

1. Why do you think there are so many schools in the area?
2. What activities might be held in the local community centre?
3. Why are the hedgerows along the railway line and the Royal Canal protected by law?
4. List three reasons why you would like to live in Blanchardstown.
5. List three reasons why you would not like to live in Blanchardstown.

C. Get Creative.

1. Pair work: Design a skate park. How big would it be? What special features could you have in it?
2. Draw a poster that will bring people to Blanchardstown. List all of its great activities and places of interest.

| Subject: | Geography | Strand: | Human Environments |
| Strand Unit: | People Living and Working in a Contrasting Part of Ireland |

| Subject: | Science | Strand: | Environmental Awareness and Care |
| Strand Unit: | Environmental Awareness |

Unit 6: Staying in Touch

New Words

carrier pigeon	Pony Express	communicate	microphone	Morse Code	online	tweet

Carrier Pigeons

A pigeon can carry about 75 grammes (which is the weight of a few sheets of paper) on its back. If you take a pigeon away from its home and release it, it will be able to find its way home again.

HOW DOES IT KNOW WHERE TO GO?

IT WILL GO HOME. IT'S A HOMING PIGEON.

I THINK IT WILL GET LOST, BECAUSE IT HAS NO MAP.

Pigeon Loft Bus used during World War I

Pigeons were used during wars to deliver important messages. The soldiers brought some pigeons with them into battle. If they needed help, they would tie a note to a pigeon's leg and release it. In some wars, the enemy used hawks to catch pigeons so that the messages could not be delivered.

Pony Express

In 1860, the President of America wanted to get a message to California. "It has to get there in 10 days," he said. The Pony Express was used to deliver the letter. The distance

Buffalo Bill, a famous Pony Express rider

was more than 3000 kilometres and riders on horseback carried the letter. There were 160 stations along the way. A rider rode as fast as he could from one station to the next. At every station, he got a fresh horse. When the rider got tired, he passed the letter to a new rider at a station. The trip needed 160 horses and around 20 riders. It took 10 days for the President's letter to arrive in California and another 10 days for a reply to be returned to him!

Hot History

In Ancient Greece, when the Olympic Games were over, pigeons were used to carry the names of the winners to the villages. That is why white doves are released today at the start of the Olympic Games.

Hot History

If they could afford it, anyone could use the Pony Express to send post. It cost $5 for a 15 gramme letter. $5 was a lot of money in those days.

Subject:	Geography	Strand:	Human Environments
Strand Unit:	People Living and Working... (Communications)		

Subject:	Science	Strand:	Environmental Awareness and Care
Strand Unit:	Science and the Environment		

35

Good News and Bad News

At six o'clock in the evening, the town bell began to ring. That could only mean one thing: an important message from the king. Within a few minutes, a large crowd had gathered at the town hall. The town crier was there. He was a man with a very loud voice. He needed a loud voice, as the microphone had not yet been invented!

"Hear Ye, Hear Ye," he called out. "I have an important message from the king. There is good news and bad news. The good news is that the king has ordered that every person in the kingdom is to have a day off."

The crowd began cheering with delight. Then a small girl called out, "Which day?"

The town crier went very red in the face.

"That's the bad news," he said. "It's today! I was meant to tell you yesterday."

WHY DIDN'T THE TOWN CRIER JUST PIN UP THE NOTICE?

BECAUSE ALMOST NO ONE WAS ABLE TO READ!

Word-of-mouth

If you want to let people in your community know that an event (a sale of work or a big match) is coming up, how would you do it? You might make a poster and have it copied. You might pin the copies up where people can see them. You may see posters about lost dogs and cats in your community. News spreads by word-of-mouth. This means that people tell one another. If there is an important event coming up, you could put an advertisement in your local newspaper. Some newspapers are delighted to hear about local news and they might even write a piece about the event and put it on the front page. Sometimes a publisher charges a customer money to place an advertisement.

Activities

A. Anwer the Questions.

1. What birds are released at the start of the Olympic Games?
2. What type of pigeon brings messages to others?
3. Buffalo _____ was a famous rider in the Pony Express.
4. A message is sent by word-of-_____ if it is spread by people.
5. Do you think that you can rely on word-of-mouth messages?

B. Make a Poster.

Make an advertisement like the one in the picture on the right, telling people about a sale of work. When you make a poster, remember to tell people where and when the event is taking place.

FAMILY FUN DAY
SUNDAY JUNE 12th
BOUNCY CASTLE
CANDY FLOSS
PLANT SALE
FACE PAINTING
FANCY DRESS AND
LOTS MORE!
PARISH HALL 3 PM
ADMISSION FREE

Local Radio

A local radio station is one that can be heard in the area close by. The radio signals do not travel very far. Every county in Ireland has a local radio station.

Kids' Talk Show with DJ Flash
"I'll finish your sentence!"

DJ Flash: Hi there. Who's on the line?

Sue: It's Sue and I want to talk to the listeners about alarm bells con…

DJ Flash: Continuing to ring? Go ahead, Sue, you're live on the air.

Sue: I was doing my homework yesterday and my neighbour's alarm was ringing for ages. I couldn't con…

DJ Flash: Concentrate?

Sue: Yeah, concentrate. I got three sums wrong.

DJ Flash: Did you not ask your mum to speak to the neighbour?

Sue: Don't be silly! My neighbour was out. The alarm wouldn't have been ringing if he was there.

DJ Flash: I meant later. Did your mum not pop over to your neighbour later?

Sue: No, Mum had to go out. I just think it's not very con…

DJ Flash: Considerate?

Sue: Yeah, considerate. It's like the alarm was out of con…

DJ Flash: Control?

Sue: Yeah, control. By the way, great show, Flash. I think you should be con…

DJ Flash: Congratulated? Thanks, Sue. Okay, now we have to con…

Sue: Conclude?

DJ Flash: Nope, converse with another listener. Hi Con…

Conor: Conor here. Hi Flash.

Hot History

Radio was invented by lots of people such as Guglielmo Marconi, Nikola Tesla, Heinrich Hertz and a few others. The first radio station in Ireland was named 2RN and it began work in 1925. It is now called RTÉ.

Hot History

The first radios could only send messages as dots and dashes in a code known as Morse Code. In 1900, Reginald Fessenden sent the first voice message by radio: "Hello, test, one, two, three, four."

Hot History

There was a radio on board the *Titanic*. When the crew of the *Titanic* realised the ship was going to sink, they used the ship's radio to send a CQD signal. The CQD signal means a ship is in distress. They got no response, so they sent an SOS ('save our souls'). The nearest ship was the *Californian*, but its radio was switched off, because the operator had gone to bed.

| Subject: | Geography | Strand: | Human Environments |
| Strand Unit: | People Living and Working... (Communications) | | |

| Subject: | Science | Strand: | Environmental Awareness and Care |
| Strand Unit: | Science and the Environment | | |

37

The Modern Way – Online

If you have a computer that is connected to the internet, you can communicate online. You can send emails to anyone else with a computer. You can also do many other things, for example:

- Ava took lots of photographs with her camera. She put them on her computer and emailed them to a printing shop. The shop printed her photographs and posted them to her.
- Gavin booked a flight from Cork to Paris online.
- Lucy wanted to learn how to make a kite. She went online and found lots of web pages about kites.
- Mark has a friend who lives in New Zealand. Mark and his friend use the internet to make their phone calls and it is very cheap.

Texts and Tweets

Mobile phone

Texts are short messages that you can send to your friends using a mobile phone. Some people like to tell all of their friends what they are up to. They even tell people who are not their friends! They write a message on their computer and it is sent by Twitter to anyone who is interested. This is called a tweet. A tweet can have up to 140 letters or digits.

Other Ways of Communicating

- **Make a Call:** Alexander Bell spoke the words, "Mr Watson, come here, I want to see you" into the first telephone in 1876. Mr Watson, who was in another room, must also have had a telephone! Today, we have mobile phones, which make it very easy for us to communicate when we are out and about.

- **Send a Letter:** The postal service has been around for hundreds of years. It used to be the only way to send a message to a far away place. The first sticky stamp was sold in 1840 and it was called the 'Penny Black'. Before that, letters were stamped with ink. Email allows us to send a message instantly.

- **Use a Sign:** People who are unable to speak or hear may use sign language. They communicate with their hands.

Sign meaning 'okay'

- **Turn on the Intercom:** Many schools, shops and offices have an intercom. The principal may speak into a microphone and his or her voice can be heard in the classrooms.

- **Buy a Newspaper:** Many newspapers are printed daily, bringing news and photos to lots of people. Many people now choose to read newspapers online using a computer or electronic tablet instead of in print.

Electronic tablet

Subject:	Geography	Strand:	Human Environments
Strand Unit:	People Living and Working... (Communications)		

Subject:	Science	Strand:	Environmental Awareness and Care
Strand Unit:	Science and the Environment		

Design and Make: A String Telephone

You will need: Two paper cups, a long roll of string
Method:

1. Use a pencil to carefully poke a hole in the bottom of each cup.

2. Thread the end of the string through the hole and tie a knot to stop it from slipping out.

3. Do the same with the other cup and the other end of the string.

4. Give one cup to a friend and stand as far away as the string will allow. Make sure the string is pulled tightly.

5. Speak into your cup while your friend holds the other cup to her/his ear.

Tests:

• Does your telephone work if the string is not tight?

• Does your telephone work if the string is touching something?

Activities

A. Fill in the Blanks.

1. A _____ radio station is heard by people in the community.

2. Online computers are connected to the _____.

3. People who are unable to speak or hear may use _____ language.

B. Find the Mistake in Each Sentence. Write the Sentence Correctly.

1. TV was invented by Marconi, Tesla and Hertz.

2. Ireland's first radio station was called 2RM.

3. Using a computer to make phone calls is very expensive.

4. A tweet has at least 140 letters or digits.

5. The *Titanic* was unable to send an SOS before it sank.

6. The telephone service has been around for hundreds of years.

C. Answer the Questions.

1. Can you name a local radio station?

2. Name your three favourite websites.

3. How many newspapers can you think of? Write their names.

4. Write a tweet telling people about your favourite film. (Remember: No more than 140 letters or digits.)

| Subject: | Geography | Strand: | Human Environments |
| Strand Unit: | People Living and Working... (Communications) | | |

| Subject: | Science | Strand: | Environmental Awareness and Care |
| Strand Unit: | Science and the Environment | | |

39

Aerial Photograph of Ballysadare, County Sligo

Map of Ballysadare, County Sligo

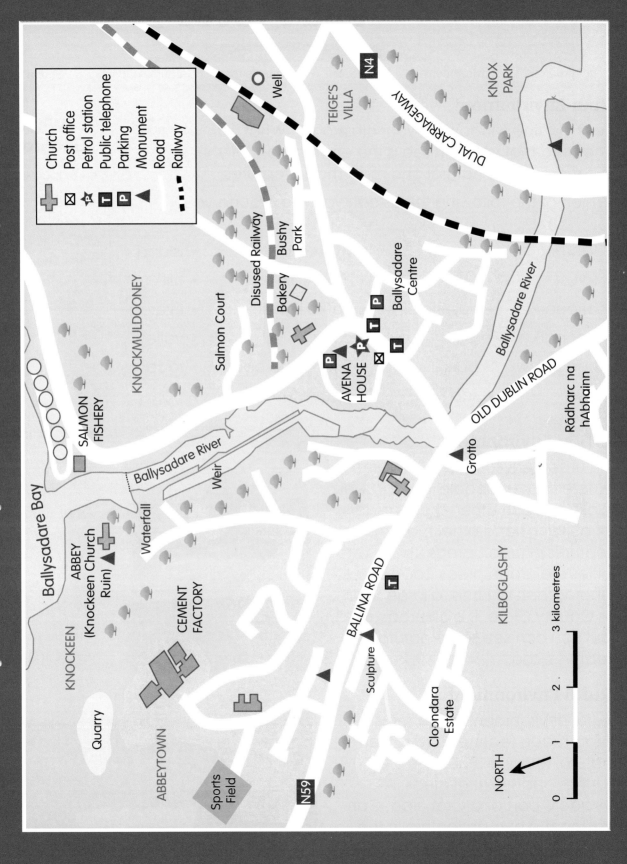

Church

Post office

Petrol station

Public telephone

Parking

Monument

Road

Railway

KNOX PARK

N4

TEIGE'S VILLA

DUAL CARRIAGEWAY

Well

Ballysadare River

Ballysadare Centre

P

T

P

T

AVENA HOUSE

OLD DUBLIN ROAD

Rádharc na hAbhainn

Grotto

Bushy Park

Bakery

Disused Railway

Salmon Court

KNOCKMULDOONEY

SALMON FISHERY

Ballysadare Bay

Ballysadare River

Weir

Waterfall

ABBEY (Knockeen Church Ruin)

KNOCKEEN

Quarry

CEMENT FACTORY

ABBEYTOWN

Sports Field

N59

BALLINA ROAD

Sculpture

T

Cloondara Estate

KILBOGLASHY

NORTH

0   1   2   3 kilometres

Unit 7: Ireland – People and Places

New Words

| geographer | environment | North Star | compass rose | county council | Shannon Estuary |

Your Environment

Look out the windows of your classroom. What can you see? The area that you can see is the environment of your school. It is made up of natural and man-made features.

Which of the following things can you see around you?

- factory
- shop
- waterfall
- island
- forest
- church
- mountain
- hill
- bridge
- hospital
- traffic lights
- river
- car park
- lake
- cave
- valley
- hedgerow
- park
- telephone box
- road
- bog
- sea
- apartment
- port

Urban Environment

An urban environment is an area where a lot of people live and work close to each other. There are lots of buildings and other man-made features in urban areas. Towns and cities are urban areas. Look at the photograph of Ennis, a large town in County Clare. It is an urban area, but you can see some natural features, too.

Ennis, County Clare

Rural Environment

Rural environments have fewer man-made features and more natural features. Buildings are farther apart in rural areas. A village is part of a rural area. Can you spot a human feature in the photograph of rural County Clare?

Rural County Clare

What Is Geography?

Geography is the study of places and the people who live there. A geographer studies those things. Geographers ask lots of questions, such as:

- Is there water?
- Is the land low or high?
- What is the weather like?
- Is the soil good for growing things?
- What kinds of rock are there?
- What kinds of plants and animals are there?
- How do people affect the environment?

| **Subject:** Geography | **Strand:** Human Environments | **Subject:** Science | **Strand:** Environmental Awareness and Care |
| **Strand Unit:** People Living and Working in a Contrasting Part of Ireland | | **Strand Unit:** Environmental Awareness | |

Photographs

Photographs can tell us a lot about a place. An aerial photograph might be taken from an aeroplane. Nowadays, we also have satellite photographs taken from space. Old photographs can show us how a place has changed over time.

What do the following four photographs of Killaloe in County Clare tell you about it?

Maps

Geographers make maps to help others to find their way around. A map shows an aerial view of a place. Symbols and colours are used to show important

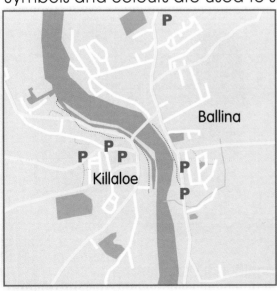

features. Blue areas are usually water features such as rivers and lakes. Dark green usually shows parks, fields and forests. You can see the roads coloured yellow and white on the street map of Killaloe. What do you think the letter P on the map represents?

| Subject: | Geography | Strand: | Human Environments |
| Strand Unit: | People Living and Working in a Contrasting Part of Ireland |

| Subject: | Science | Strand: | Environmental Awareness and Care |
| Strand Unit: | Environmental Awareness |

43

Major Natural Features of Ireland

Mountains

MacGillycuddy's Reeks

A mountain is a natural feature that rises high above the area that surrounds it. Mountains are made from rocks and earth. Generally, mountains are higher than 600 metres. Hills are lower than 600 metres. The centre of Ireland is mainly flatland, except for the Slieve Bloom Mountains and the Silvermines. Ireland's highest mountain is Carrauntoohil in the MacGillycuddy's Reeks in County Kerry. Ireland's mountains are low-lying compared to mountains such as the Alps in Europe.

Seas and Oceans

A sea or ocean is a very large body of salt water. Ireland is an island, which means that it is surrounded by water. The Irish Sea and the North Channel separate us from our nearest neighbours in Britain. The Atlantic Ocean separates Ireland from America.

Atlantic Ocean at County Clare

Rivers and Lakes

Lough Neagh

A river is a large body of fresh water. A lake is a large body of fresh water surrounded by land. Some rivers flow into and out of lakes. Most rivers flow into the sea. The longest river in Ireland is the River Shannon, which stretches from County Cavan in Ulster, down to the sea at County Limerick. Ireland's largest lake is Lough Neagh in Ulster. Lough Neagh is also larger than any lake in Britain.

Activities

Look at the Map on Page 29. Answer the Questions.

1. Name three lakes on the River Shannon.
2. Which lake is the largest in Ireland?
3. Name the ocean to the west of Ireland.
4. Name the sea to the east of Ireland.
5. Name a river just north of the River Lee.
6. Name a river just south of the River Lee.
7. Name a river that starts in the Wicklow Mountains.
8. Name a river that starts in the Mourne Mountains.
9. On which river will you find Lough Erne?
10. Name three 'sister' rivers that flow into the sea together at Waterford.

Subject:	Geography	Strand:	Human Environments
Strand Unit:	People Living and Working in a Contrasting Part of Ireland		

Subject:	Science	Strand:	Environmental Awareness and Care
Strand Unit:	Environmental Awareness		

Provinces and Counties of Ireland

The map below shows the provinces and counties of Ireland.

Ireland is divided into four large regions called provinces. The provinces are: Connacht, Ulster, Leinster and Munster. The largest province is Munster and the smallest province is Connacht. Leinster has the greatest number of people, because it includes our capital city, Dublin. Connacht has the smallest population. Each province has its own crest and rugby team.

Each province is divided into smaller areas called counties. There are twelve counties in Leinster, nine in Ulster, six in Munster and five in Connacht. Ulster includes the six counties of Northern Ireland and three other counties that are part of the Republic of Ireland. The largest county is Cork and the smallest is Louth. County Dublin has the largest population of all the counties. Leitrim has the smallest population. Each county has its own crest and Gaelic football team.

| Subject: | Geography | Strand: | Human Environments | | Subject: | Science | Strand: | Environmental Awareness and Care |
| Strand Unit: | People Living and Working in a Contrasting Part of Ireland | | | | Strand Unit: | Environmental Awareness | | |

45

Study of a Place in Ireland: County Clare

Satellite photograph of Clare

Lough Derg

Aran Islands

Shannon Estuary

Crest of County Clare

We have already seen some photographs of places in County Clare. Let's find out more. County Clare is located on the west coast of Ireland in the province of Munster. Ennis is its main town. Look at the satellite photograph of County Clare. You can see the mountains and hills in brown and the low-lying land in green. You can see the Shannon Estuary, where the Shannon meets the Atlantic Ocean. The dark area is Lough Derg. The River Shannon links Lough Derg to the sea. The Aran Islands lie off the coasts of Clare and Galway. Famous natural features in County Clare include the Cliffs of Moher, the Aillwee Cave and the Burren. The highest point in County Clare is Moylussa (532 metres) in the Slieve Bernagh Mountains.

The Burren

Some Tourist Attractions of County Clare

Music	Castles	Lahinch Beach
County Clare is famous for traditional Irish music. Each year, famous music festivals take place in the county.	County Clare is famous for its castles such as Bunratty and Dromoland (pictured above).	Lahinch in County Clare has 2 kilometres of beach, where surfing and other water activities are popular.

Activities

A. Draw.

1. Draw symbols that you might use on a map to show each of the following features.
   (a) trees, **(b)** swimming pool, **(c)** telephone box, **(d)** mountain, **(e)** church, **(f)** fishing lake, **(g)** fire station

2. Draw a compass in your copy and explain how it works.

B. Write 'Natural' or 'Man-made' for Each of the Following Features.
   factory, river, lake, shop, traffic lights, bin, hill, forest, car park, hospital, bridge

Subject:	Geography	Strand:	Human Environments
Strand Unit:	People Living and Working in a Contrasting Part of Ireland		

Subject:	Science	Strand:	Environmental Awareness and Care
Strand Unit:	Environmental Awareness		

Unit 8: Mountains

magma   crust   range   lava   Sherpa   summit   altitude   coniferous   feral   terrace   scree   erosion

The Earth's Layers

The red part in the centre of the Earth is made of solid iron.
The orange part is made of liquid iron. The yellow part is
made of hot liquid rock called magma. The blue and green
layer is the Earth's crust – the part where we live.

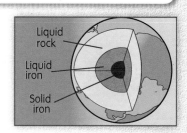

Liquid rock
Liquid iron
Solid iron

YOU MIGHT THINK
THAT THE EARTH IS
JUST A BIG LUMP
OF ROCK, BUT IT IS
ACTUALLY MADE UP
OF LAYERS!

Design and Make: A Model of the Earth's Layers

You will need: Plasticine in various colours, knife
Method:

1. Begin with a small red ball of plasticine.

2. Take a bigger ball of orange plasticine and use it to surround the red ball.

3. Take an even bigger ball of yellow plasticine and use it to surround the orange ball.

4. Surround the yellow ball with a thin layer of blue plasticine. Stick on some green plasticine for land.

5. Get an adult to cut your Earth in half. You should be able to see all of the layers.

Three Ways that Mountains Are Formed:

1. Fold Mountains

Ouch!

ASIA   INDIA

The Earth's crust is made of huge plates that
fit together like a giant jigsaw. The plates
float on the liquid rock beneath them. They
are always moving and can sometimes
bump into each other. Sometimes, when
two plates push against each other, the rock is forced
upwards into a fold mountain. The tallest mountains on
Earth are fold mountains. About 50 million years ago, the
plate carrying India bumped into the plate carrying the rest of Asia. Asia's plate
said "Hey, watch where you're going!" but India's plate kept pushing. The edge
of the Asian plate was forced upwards into a great mountain range called the
Himalayas. A group of mountains is called a mountain range. To see how a fold
mountain is made, put two of your copy books flat on your desk. Imagine that they
are two plates. Now push them into each other and see what happens.

Hot Geography

The Himalaya
Mountains grow
about
6 centimetres
every year, because
the two plates are
still pushing into
each other.

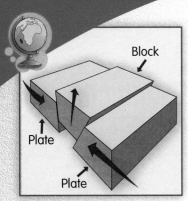

2. Block Mountains

Sometimes when two plates push into each other, a block of rock breaks off one of the plates. The block of rock is forced up between the two plates. This is called a block mountain. Block mountains are usually flat on top and they often have steep sides.

Yosemite Valley, Sierra Nevada Mountains, California is an example of block mountains

3. Volcanoes

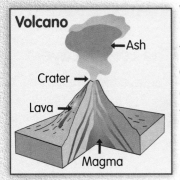

When magma comes out of a volcano, we call it lava. When lava cools, it hardens into rock and forms a cone-shaped mountain. As this volcano continues to erupt, more lava pours down its surface and hardens. As the layers of hardened lava build up, the mountain increases in size.

Gunung Bromo Volcano, Indonesia

Activities

1. Look at the maps of Ireland on pages 28–29. Write the names of the counties where the following mountains are located. **(a)** Slieve Mish Mountains, **(b)** MacGillycuddy's Reeks, **(c)** Mourne Mountains, **(d)** Nephin Beg Mountains, **(e)** Maumturk Mountains

2. Draw a diagram of a volcano and include the labels below.
   Lava, Magma, Crater, Ash

3. In your own words and using pictures, explain how block and fold mountains are made.

Tall Mountains

The Andes is the longest mountain range in the world. It stretches from the top to the bottom of South America. The tallest mountain range in the world is the Himalayas. Mount Everest, the highest mountain peak in the world, is in the Himalayas. Ireland's tallest mountain is Carrauntoohil. It is part of a mountain range called the MacGillycuddy's Reeks, in County Kerry. Carrauntoohil is 1038 metres tall and it can be climbed without having to use climbing equipment. Walkers must be careful though, because the weather changes very quickly on a mountain. It might be fine and dry at the bottom, but at the top it could be wet, cold, windy or snowy. Climbers should always check the weather forecast and bring the correct equipment when climbing a mountain.

Carrauntoohil

Subject: Geography **Strand:** Natural Environments
Strand Unit: The Local Natural Environment

Subject: Science **Strand:** Environmental Awareness and Care
Strand Unit: Environmental Awareness

Mount Everest

At 8848 metres, Mount Everest is more than eight times taller than Ireland's highest mountain. It is on the border between Nepal and Tibet. Its rocky summit is covered in deep snow all year round. With winds faster than 300 kilometres per hour and temperatures as low as −60 °C, you would expect that nobody wants to go there. However, in the past 60 years, more than 5000 people have climbed to the top! Because the mountain is so tall, there is very little oxygen at the summit (top) and climbers suffer from altitude sickness. So far, 227 people have died while climbing Mount Everest. Most of their bodies are still there. In 1953, Sir Edmund Hillary and his Sherpa guide, Tenzing Norgay, were the first people to climb to the summit. The Sherpas are a people who live in the Himalayas.

Sir Edmund Hillary and Tenzing Norgay

Mount Everest

A Trick Question!

Ask your parents, 'Who was the first person to place two feet on Mount Everest?' You know that parents love showing off how clever they are, so they will probably say, 'Edmund Hillary' or 'Tenzing Norgay'. You can tell them that it was in fact, Radhanath Sikdar, a mathematician who measured the peak at 29,000 feet. However, he thought that people would not believe it was exactly 29,000 feet, so he added 2 feet to make it 29,002. This is how he became the first person to place 'two feet' on Mount Everest!

Hot Geography

Olympus Mons, a volcano on Mars, is 22,500 metres tall. That is almost three times taller than Mount Everest!

Another Trick Question!

What is the world's tallest mountain? 'Mount Everest,' you might say. However, Mount Everest is only the tallest mountain on land. The tallest mountain in the world is in fact underwater. Mauna Kea measures 10,203 metres from its base in the Pacific Ocean to the volcano at its summit, on the island of Hawaii.

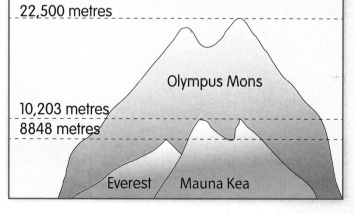

22,500 metres
Olympus Mons
10,203 metres
8848 metres
Everest   Mauna Kea

Subject:	Geography	Strand:	Natural Environments
Strand Unit:	The Local Natural Environment		

Subject:	Science	Strand:	Environmental Awareness and Care
Strand Unit:	Environmental Awareness		

Mountain Plants

If you climb a mountain, you will see that the plants growing on the bottom of the mountain are very different from those growing at the top. Broad-leaf trees such as beech and oak can grow on the lower slopes, but not higher up, where the air is cold and thin. Coniferous trees can survive on the higher slopes because their leaves are tough and their trunks have thick bark to protect them from strong winds. Mountain plants have strong roots, short stems and small flowers that grow close to the ground, allowing them to survive the strong winds.

Sweet Alison is a hardy mountain plant that can grow in a thin layer of soil

Mountain Animals

Most animals could not survive on mountains, but wild or feral goats are well suited to life on Irish mountains. They have long, shaggy coats to protect them from the cold and they are not fussy eaters. Feral goats are very agile and they can jump onto narrow cliff ledges to reach plants and shrubs. They have great balance and their hooves are good for clinging to rocks.

Feral goat

Tourism

During spring and summer, tourists love to walk and climb in the mountains. During the winter, some mountains are popular places for skiers. Hotels, cable cars and ski lifts are built especially for skiing holidays.

Ski lifts

Mining

Many mountains are mined to collect slate, coal, gold and other metals. The Silvermine Mountains in Tipperary were mined for copper, lead, zinc and of course, silver. Can you find the Silvermines on the map on page 29?

Keeper Hill, Silvermine Mountains

Mountain People

Bad weather and rocky slopes make life in the mountains difficult. However, the Sherpas of Nepal are experts at surviving in the Himalaya Mountains. There are no roads, so Sherpas carry everything on their backs. They are expert porters and guides for the visitors who climb Mount Everest.

Sherpas carrying goods

It is difficult to grow crops on steep slopes, so the Nepalese farmers cut terraces into the mountains to create flat ground and to stop the soil from being washed down the side of the mountain.

Rice terraces in Nepal

Subject: Geography Strand: Natural Environments
Strand Unit: The Local Natural Environment

Subject: Science Strand: Environmental Awareness and Care
Strand Unit: Environmental Awareness

Mountain Erosion

Mountains get worn away, or eroded, by rivers, people and animals. Wind and rain also wear away the surface of a mountain. Rainwater gets into the cracks in the rocks. When it freezes, it turns into ice and gets bigger, causing pieces of loose rock to break away. The loose rock is called scree. Walkers and climbers can also damage mountains by knocking the scree down to the bottom of the mountain.

Scree on Croagh Patrick, County Mayo

Rivers wash away stones and pebbles from a mountain, slowly

V-shaped valley

eroding it. Over a long period of time, a river can even cut a V-shaped valley into a mountain.

Plants and trees help to hold the soil together on a mountainside. If too many trees are cut down, or if animals eat all of the plants, the soil will be washed away by the rain.

Soil erosion

Activities

A. Find the Mistake in Each Sentence. Write the Sentence Correctly.

1. Liquid iron is called magma.
2. The highest mountain in the world is Carrauntoohil.
3. The loose rock on the sides of a mountain is called Sherpa.
4. Olympus Mons is the highest volcano on Earth.
5. The longest mountain range in the world is the Himalaya Mountains.

B. Look at the Maps on Pages 28–29. Write the Mountains that are in the Following Counties.

1. Kerry
2. Wicklow
3. Donegal
4. Galway
5. Mayo
6. Down

C. Who or What Am I?

1. Everybody thinks Mount Everest is the tallest mountain on this planet, but I am even taller.
2. I climbed to the top of Mount Everest along with Tenzing Norgay.
3. I am a hardy mountain plant with a white flower.
4. I am a group of people who live in the Himalayas.

D. Get Creative.

How many mountains or mountain ranges in Ireland or the world can you match to letters of the alphabet? (For example, A for Andes, B for Blackstairs Mountains.)

Map of Great Britain and Northern Ireland

Orkney Islands

Shetland Islands

Outer Hebrides

NORTH WEST HIGHLANDS

Loch Ness

Loch Lomond

Ben Nevis

Aberdeen

GRAMPIAN MTS.

Dundee

R. Clyde

Glasgow

Edinburgh

SCOTLAND

SOUTHERN UPLANDS

NORTH ATLANTIC OCEAN

NORTHERN IRELAND

Belfast

Newcastle

R. Tyne

R. Tees

PENNINES

NORTH SEA

REPUBLIC OF IRELAND

IRISH SEA

ISLE OF MAN

R. Ouse

R. Aire

Liverpool

Manchester

R. Mersey

Mount Snowdon

WALES

R. Trent

Birmingham

ENGLAND

CAMBRIAN MTS.

R. Severn

R. Avon

Great Ouse

Cardiff

Swansea

R. Thames

London

CELTIC SEA

R. Tamar

ISLE OF WIGHT

ENGLISH CHANNEL

GUERNSEY

JERSEY

FRANCE

0 50 100 150
Kilometres

Map of Egypt

53

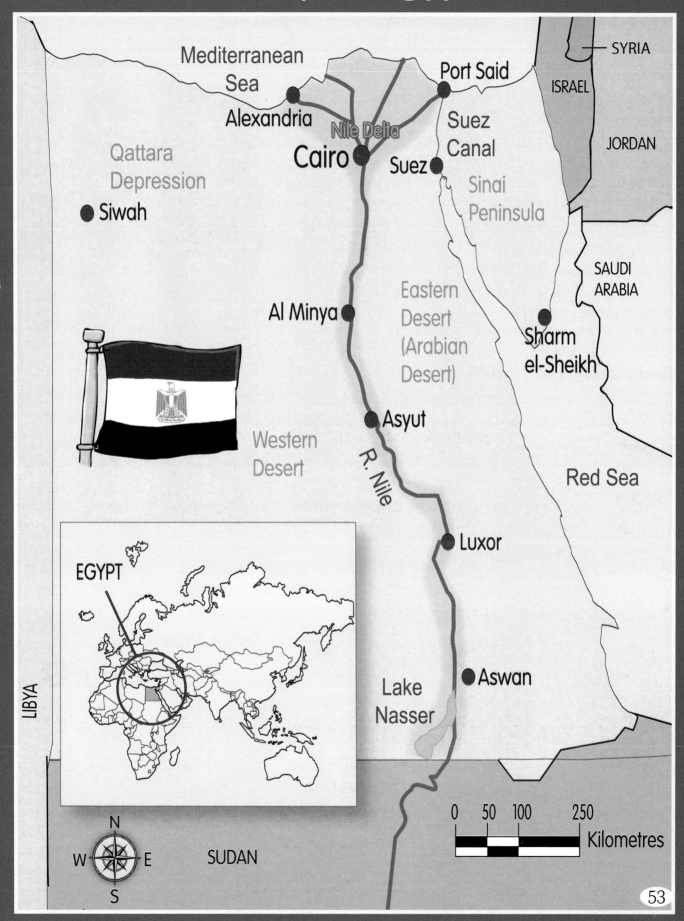

Mediterranean Sea

Port Said

SYRIA

ISRAEL

Alexandria

Nile Delta

Suez Canal

JORDAN

Qattara Depression

Cairo

Suez

Siwah

Sinai Peninsula

SAUDI ARABIA

Al Minya

Eastern Desert (Arabian Desert)

Sharm el-Sheikh

Asyut

Western Desert

R. Nile

Red Sea

Luxor

EGYPT

Lake Nasser

Aswan

LIBYA

N

W   E

S

SUDAN

0   50 100   250

Kilometres

Unit 9: Britain

Where Is Britain?

Britain is located off the north-west coast of Europe. It is also called Great Britain, the United Kingdom or the UK. Britain is made up of three countries called Scotland, England and Wales. Great Britain does not include Northern Ireland, but the the UK does. London is the capital city of Britain and it is located in the south-east of England. Britain is an island, so it is surrounded by water. It lies between the North Atlantic Ocean and the North Sea. Ireland and France are located nearby. Britain is about 40 kilometres from France. The two countries are linked by the Channel Tunnel.

Geography and Nature

The weather and the countryside of Britain are similar to those of Ireland. Much of Scotland and Wales are covered with highlands and mountain ranges with valleys in between. Much of Central England is flatland or else covered with low-lying hills. Britain is dotted with deep, narrow lakes. The Lake District in North-west England is a very popular tourist spot. The area is famous for its high mountains and beautiful lakes. In Scotland, the lakes are called lochs. The most famous lake in Britain is Loch Ness in Scotland. Rumour has it that a giant monster called Nessie lives in Loch Ness. Watch out if you ever visit!

Quick Facts

Capital:	London Flag:
Population:	60 million
Official languages:	English, Welsh
Money:	pound sterling
Longest river:	Severn
Other major rivers:	Thames and Tyne
Tallest mountain:	Ben Nevis, Scotland

Subject: Geography **Strand:** Human Environments
Strand Unit: People and Other Lands

Hot History

Henry Tudor

Britain was once covered with thick forest, just as Ireland was. Early settlers cleared the forests for farming. The first settlers arrived in Britain about 10,000 years ago. The Celts arrived about 3000 years ago and they forced the first settlers to move up to Scotland. The Romans invaded about 2000 years ago. They improved the services in Britain by building roads, bathhouses and sewers. Towards the end of the 1400s, Henry Tudor from Wales became the first of the Tudor kings. Many important kings and queens have ruled Britain since then.

Hot History

By the 1800s, Britain was one of the most powerful countries in the world. Many explorers and traders from Britain travelled the world and discovered new lands. They often claimed ownership of the new lands. Britain ruled many countries throughout the world. They were called colonies and they included Ireland, India, Australia, New Zealand, South Africa and the United States. Those countries are no longer ruled by Britain, as they won their independence.

■ Former British colonies

Houses of Parliament

10 Downing Street

Government

The government of Britain has changed many times over the years. Kings once ruled Britain and its colonies. The British Government now rules Britain. It is made up of Members of Parliament (MPs). They are elected by the people and they meet in the Houses of Parliament in Westminster. Nowadays, a king or queen has no real power and cannot make the law. The leader of the Government is called the Prime Minister. The Prime Minister of Britain lives in 10 Downing Street in London.

Hot History

In May 2011, Queen Elizabeth II paid a state visit to the Republic of Ireland. This was the first visit to Ireland by a British king or queen since 1911, when Ireland was ruled by Great Britain.

Activities

1. Explain the difference between Britain and the United Kingdom.
2. Describe Britain's weather.
3. How did the Romans improve life in Britain?
4. What historic event took place in 2011?
5. Where does the Prime Minister of Britain live?

Hot History

William Shakespeare is one of the most famous playwrights of all time. He was born in England in 1564. He wrote many plays including Romeo and Juliet, Macbeth and King Lear.

Hot History

JK Rowling was born in England in 1965. She is the author of the Harry Potter series of books. She lives in Edinburgh, Scotland.

JK Rowling

Sports and Leisure

Britain is well-known for sport. Many of Ireland's most popular games were first played in Britain. These include soccer, rugby, tennis, golf, boxing and cricket.

Soccer	Tennis
 Soccer is the most popular sport in Britain and it has been played for hundreds of years. Some of England's teams are Manchester United, Liverpool, Arsenal and Chelsea.	The world's most famous tennis championship takes place in England each year. Players from all over the world take part in the Wimbledon Championships. Millions of people watch at home on television.
Horse-racing	Golf
 Horse-racing is a very popular sport in Britain and race meetings are held throughout the year. Some of the best-known horse races are held at Cheltenham, Ascot and Epsom.	 It is said that Scotland is the home of golf. There are nearly 600 registered golf courses in Scotland – that is nearly twice as many as there are in Ireland. The most famous golf course is Saint Andrew's, near Dundee.

British Industries

Britain has many different industries, including the motor industry, farming, fishing, tourism and energy. Let's find out more about British industries and meet some of the people who work in them.

Subject: Geography   Strand: Human Environments
Strand Unit: People and Other Lands

Energy Industry

Britain has large amounts of coal, oil and gas. Wales and England have many coalmines and in the past, children were sent down into the mines to bring up the coal. Today, a cable from Rush in Dublin travels under the sea to Wales, carrying electricity between Ireland and Britain. This is called the interconnector.

HELLO, MY NAME IS JOHN. I WORK AS A WELDER ON AN OIL RIG OFF THE COAST OF SCOTLAND. I WORK FOR SIX WEEKS AT A TIME AND THEN I RETURN HOME TO EDINBURGH TO SEE MY FAMILY. LIFE ON THE OIL RIG CAN BE TOUGH, ESPECIALLY IN WINTER WHEN THE WEATHER IS HARSH AND THE SEA IS ROUGH.

HI, MY NAME IS JOY AND THE INSET PICTURE IS OF MY BROTHER, FRASER. I WORK IN A HOLIDAY CAMP IN WALES, OR CYMRU, AS IT IS KNOWN IN WELSH. MY BROTHER WORKS AS A BAGGAGE HANDLER AT HEATHROW, BRITAIN'S LARGEST AND BUSIEST AIRPORT.

Tourism Industry

Britain is a popular choice for many tourists. Wales is well known for Mount Snowdon, its highest mountain. The mountain is popular with rock climbers and hillwalkers. It was there that Edmund Hillary trained before climbing Mount Everest.

Farming

Many farms in Britain are larger than those in Ireland, but not quite as big as the mega farms in America. Farmers rear sheep and cattle and grow crops like those grown in Ireland.

HELLO, MY NAME IS MOIRA. I'M A SHEEP FARMER IN NORTHERN SCOTLAND. I LIVE IN THE SHADOW OF THE GRAMPIAN MOUNTAINS, SO MUCH OF MY LAND IS SPREAD OVER HILLS AND VALLEYS. THIS TYPE OF LAND IS PERFECT FOR SHEEP FARMING. IN SUMMER, THE SHEEP ARE SHORN FOR THEIR WOOL. PEOPLE USE IT TO MAKE CLOTHES AND RUGS.

Banking

HI, MY NAME IS ALICE. I WORK IN A BANK IN LONDON. I LIVE IN ASCOT AND I TRAVEL TO WORK BY TRAIN EACH MORNING. ON MY WAY TO WORK, I PASS SOME OF THE MOST FAMOUS SIGHTS IN LONDON, SUCH AS THE LONDON EYE AND BIG BEN.

Big Ben with London Eye in background

Subject:	Geography	Strand:	Human Environments
Strand Unit:	People and Other Lands		

57

Food

British food is similar to Irish food. Roast beef with Yorkshire pudding is a traditional British Sunday lunch. Britain is famous for its fish and chips, which often come wrapped in newspaper from the chip-shop. British people have unusual names for some of their favourite meals. Bubble and squeak is made from leftover vegetables. The main vegetables are potato and cabbage, but any vegetable can be used. The cold mixture is fried on a pan. This dish gets its name from the sound that is made when it is cooking. Bangers and mash is another favourite. 'Bangers' are actually sausages. During the World Wars, meat was scarce, so sausages often contained a lot of water. They often exploded with a bang as they were cooked!

Bubble and squeak cakes

Activities

1. Choose three of the people from this unit. Write three sentences about each of them.

2. Out of the industries that were discussed, which one would you like to work in and why?

3. Write a paragraph about Irish food, including some Irish favourites.

4. There are two different types of map shown below. **(a)** In what ways are the maps the same? **(b)** In what ways are they different?

Subject: Geography   **Strand:** Human Environments
Strand Unit: People and Other Lands

Unit 10: Science and the World Around Us

Timeline

- 1898 Marie Curie discovers polonium and radium

- 1900 John Phillip Holland sells submarine design to the American Navy

- 1903 Mary Anderson invents the windscreen wiper

- 1909 Harry Ferguson makes Ireland's first powered flight

- 1925 John Logie Baird transmits moving pictures

- 1940s Alan Turing designs the first modern computer

Science and Technology

Imagine a world without lights, telephones, medicine, cars, computers, internet, television and DVDs! Our knowledge of all living and non-living things comes from science. Look around your classroom and school and you will notice that almost every object is based on science and technology. Look at the timeline to see some of the inventors that you will meet in this unit.

Scientists

Most scientists work in laboratories, hospitals, factories, mines, offices and research centres. However, you can find scientists working almost anywhere. Scientists are always testing materials to find new discoveries that will make our lives better. When scientists are trying something new, they start by coming up with an idea. Next, they investigate and check their idea. It is very important for scientists to record the results of their experiments, because they might make a big discovery or invent something new. You do not need to be a scientist to invent something, but you do need to have an idea and to test your idea. Let's take a look at some inventions that have helped to make the world a better place.

Recording results

Hi, my name is Mary Anderson. I was born in Alabama in the USA in 1866. In 1902, I visited New York. I noticed that motorists had to open their car windows when it rained, in order to see the road! I thought that there had to be a better way to drive in the rain. When I returned home, I started to work on a solution to this problem. I came up with a device with a swinging arm attached to a rubber blade. The device was operated from inside the vehicle, by pushing a lever like a door handle, back and forth. I called it the windscreen wiper.

Mary Anderson
1866–1953

Marie Curie
1867–1934

Bonjour, je m'appelle Madame Curie. I was born in Poland in 1867, but I spent much of my life in France. I always dreamed of becoming a scientist, but my family could not afford to send me to university. When I was 18 years old, I became a nanny. I used my pay to help my sister to go to university. Later, she helped to pay for my education. I studied at the Sorbonne University in Paris to become a chemist. I met my husband, Pierre, there. We discovered two metals called radium and polonium. We found that those metals could be used to help treat people who had cancer.

Hello my name is John Logie Baird. I was born in Scotland in 1888 and I studied at the University of Glasgow. I was interested in making an object that could show pictures on a screen. I invented 'TV'! In 1925, I received the world's first television pictures in my laboratory. My test object was a dummy called 'Stooky Bill'. I placed him in front of the camera and I was really excited when the image of the dummy appeared on my screen. I was even more excited when I was able to see moving pictures on the screen!

John Logie Baird
1888–1946

| Subject: | Science | Strand: | Environmental Awareness and Care |
| Strand Unit: | Science and the Environment | | |

Alan Turing
1912-1954

Hello, my name is Alan Turing. I was born in London, England in 1912. During my life, I worked as a mathematician and a computer scientist. Many people agree that I designed the first modern computer. However, that's not to say that I invented the first computer. The Sumerians invented the first computer way back in 2700 BC, when they started using the abacus! Today, there are many types of computer – laptops, tablets and interactive whiteboards. Believe it or not, the first 'modern' computers back in the 1940s were the size of a large room!

Activities

A. Who Am I?

1. I received the world's first television pictures in 1925.
2. Many people agree that I designed the first modern computer.
3. I was born in Poland in 1867.
4. It would be difficult to drive safely without my invention.

B. Get Creative.

1. Look around your classroom. Make a list of five things that we have due to the work of inventors. (For example, light bulbs.)
2. Which of the four inventors do you think made the most important discovery? Give reasons for your answer.

Irish Inventors

Irish people have also taken an interest in science and technology. Many Irish women and men have invented objects that have changed the world.

Hello, my name is John Philip Holland. I was born in County Clare in 1840. My family moved to Limerick after my father died. I went to school in Limerick and I became a teacher. I moved to the USA in 1873. I was always very interested in science and travel, especially sea travel. Have you ever read a book that gave you a great idea? I read *Twenty Thousand Leagues Under the Sea* by Jules Verne, which is about the captain of an underwater ship. I was so excited that I decided to design a submarine. In 1900, the US Navy and the Japanese Navy bought my designs. Today, there are many submarines in the ocean; some of them are powered by nuclear energy!

John Philip Holland
1840-1914

My name is Harry Ferguson and I was born in County Down in 1884. When I was young, I spent lots of time working on my family's farm. When I was a teenager, I went to work in my brother's car and cycle shop in Belfast. I became interested in aeroplanes and in 1909, I made the first powered flight in Ireland. In 1911, I opened my own car business in Belfast. I also sold American tractors, but many Irish farmers complained that they were sometimes dangerous to operate. In 1936, I began to make my own tractors. Later on, I went into business with Massey Harris of Canada. Together we set up the Massey Ferguson company.

Harry Ferguson
1884–1960

Technology of the Future

Some inventions have helped to make our world a better place and changed the way that we do things. Did you ever wonder what inventions of the future might look like? If you are a *Star Trek* fan, you will have heard the famous phrase, 'beam me up'. Imagine if this could happen in the future!

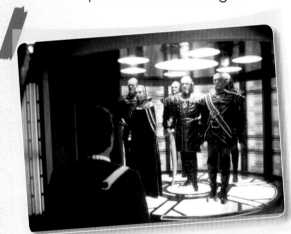

Star Trek transporter scene

The transporter would scramble your body's cells into thousands of tiny pieces and transport them to another place, where they would be put back together again!

Have you ever seen the film, *Back to the Future*? The boy in the film has a time-travel machine. Imagine if you had a time-travel machine! What would you do? Who would you like to meet? Believe it or not, scientists have experimented with time travel and some believe that it might be possible. Imagine meeting your future self!

Hot History

In 1942, the Germans launched the first rocket into space. In 1947, the first animals were launched into space, so that scientists could study the effects of space travel. Fruit flies were chosen because of their similarities to humans! Albert, the monkey, followed in 1949 and Laika, the dog, followed in 1957. In 1961, the Russian Cosmonaut, Yuri Gagarin, became the first man in space. The American astronauts Neil Armstrong and Buzz Aldrin reached the moon in 1969. In 2004, a new airline called Virgin Galactic began offering tourists flights into space.

Subject:	Science	Strand:	Environmental Awareness and Care
Strand Unit:	Science and the Environment		

Hot History

The beginnings of the internet can be traced back to 1969. Four universities in the USA created a network that linked them together to help with research. Email followed in 1972. In 1989, scientists in the CERN laboratory in Switzerland created the World Wide Web (www), which we now use.

Skycars

Scientists and mechanics have already worked on designs for flying cars! You could be driving one of those cars in the future. In 1989, one of the first successful skycars, the *M200X*, took flight. Since that time it has made 200 flights and it can reach heights of 15 metres. Some companies are working on skycars that can travel at speeds of up to 500 kilometres per hour, over long distances, without stopping to re-fuel. Imagine that some day you might be able to 'drive' to the USA!

Futuristic flying car

Activities

A. Answer the Questions.

1. Which famous Irish inventor was born in 1840?
2. Which underwater vessel did John Philip Holland invent?
3. How do we know that Harry Ferguson was interested in machinery from a young age?
4. How did the Massey Ferguson company get its name?
5. How would transporters work?

B. Get Creative.

1. Who would you like to meet if you could travel back in time? Give reasons for your answer.
2. Imagine that you are John Logie Baird and you have just invented the first working television. Write a message to your family telling them about your invention. You cannot use any more than 20 words!

C. Crack the Code.

Long ago, Morse Code was used for sending telegrams. It is made up of sequences of dots and dashes that represent letters and numbers. Crack the code to find out what Neil Armstrong said when he landed on the moon.

A •—	B —•••	C —•—•	D —••	E •	F ••—•	G ——•	H ••••	I ••
J •———	K —•—	L •—••	M ——	N —•	O ———	P •——•	Q ——•—	R •—•
S •••	T —	U ••—	V •••—	W •——	X —••—	Y —•——	Z ——••	

——• •• •— —• —   •—•• • •— •—•

••—• ——— •—   —— •— —• —•— •• —• —••

"**One small step for man, one** _____ _____ _____"

_____ "

Political Map of the World

N
W   E
S

BEAUFORT
SEA

GREENLAND

GREENLAND
SEA

NORWEGIAN
SEA

ICELAND

Alaska
(USA)

CANADA

NORTH ATLANTIC
OCEAN

UNITED
KINGDOM

DENMARK

NETHERLANDS
IRELAND

BELGIUM

PACIFIC OCEAN

UNITED STATES
OF AMERICA

FRANCE

ATLANTIC OCEAN

PORTUGAL

SPAIN

MEXICO

BAHAMAS

BELIZE

CUBA

DOMINICAN REPUBLIC

MOROCCO

TUNISIA

WESTERN
SAHARA

ALGERIA

HONDURAS

BRITISH VIRGIN ISLANDS

JAMAICA

GUATEMALA

HAITI

GUYANA

MAURITANIA

MALI

EL SALVADOR

VENEZUELA

SURINAME

SENEGAL

NICARAGUA

COSTA RICA

COLOMBIA

FRENCH
GUIANA

GAMBIA

BURKINA

Guinea
Bissau

EQUATOR

PANAMA

SIERRA
LEONE

IVORY
COAST

GALAPAGOS
IS. (ECUADOR)

ECUADOR

LIBERIA

GHANA TOGO

BEN

EQUATORI
GUINEA

PERU

BRAZIL

BOLIVIA

PARAGUAY

CHILE

ARGENTINA

URUGUAY

SOUTH ATLANTIC
OCEAN

FALKLAND
IS. (UK)

SOUTHERN OCEAN

0   1000   2000   4000 Kilometres

ARCTIC OCEAN

ARCTIC OCEAN

BARENTS
SEA

NORWAY
SWEDEN
FINLAND

RUSSIAN FEDERATION

BERING
SEA

ESTONIA
LATVIA
RUSSIA
LITHUANIA
GERMANY
BELARUS
POLAND
CZECH REP.
SLOV
AUS
HUNGARY
ITALY
UKRAINE
MOLDOVA
ROMANIA
BULGARIA
GEORGIA
TURKEY
ARMENIA
GREECE
AZERBAIJAN
CYPRUS
LEBANON
ISRAEL
SYRIA
IRAQ
KUWAIT
JORDAN
QATAR
SAUDI
ARABIA
U.A.E
YEMEN
OMAN

KAZAKHSTAN

MONGOLIA

NORTH KOREA

UZBEKISTAN
KYRGYZSTAN
TURKMENISTAN
TAJIKISTAN

CHINA

JAPAN

IRAN
AFGHANISTAN
PAKISTAN

NEPAL
BHUTAN

INDIA

BURMA

LAOS

SOUTH KOREA

TAIWAN

MACAO
VIETNAM
PHILIPPINES

BANGLADESH
THAILAND
CAMBODIA

LIBYA
EGYPT
NIGER
CHAD
SUDAN
ERITREA
ETHIOPIA
SOMALIA
UGANDA

NIGERIA
CAMEROON
CENTRAL AFRICAN REP.
RWANDA
KENYA
Dem. Rep.
Congo
BURUNDI
TANZANIA
GABON
CONGO

SRI
LANKA

EQUATOR

MALAYSIA
INDONESIA

PAPUA
NEW GUINEA

MALAWI

INDIAN OCEAN

ANGOLA
ZAMBIA
MOZAMBIQUE
MADAGASCAR
ZIMBABWE
NAMIBIA
BOTSWANA
SOUTH
AFRICA
LESOTHO

MAURITIUS

FIJI

AUSTRALIA

NEW
ZEALAND

TASMAN
SEA

SOUTHERN OCEAN

65

ANTARCTICA

Physical Map of the World

GREENLAND

AR

EUROP

Alps

Atlas Mountains

Sahara
Desert

AFRIC

R. Niger

R. Yukon

R. Mackenzie

Great Bear
Lake

Great Slave
Lake

Hudson
Bay

Rocky Mountains

NORTH
AMERICA

Great Lakes

St. Lawrence R.

R. Missouri

R. Colorado

R. Mississippi

Sierra Madre

Gulf of
Mexico

NORTH
ATLANTIC
OCEAN

Caribbean Sea

R. Orinoco

Panama
Canal

EQUATOR

R. Amazon

SOUTH
AMERICA

Lake
Titicaca

Andes Mountains

PACIFIC
OCEAN

R. Parana

SOUTH
ATLANTIC
OCEAN

0   1000 2000   4000 Kilometres

ARCTIC OCEAN

EUROPE

Lake Onega

Ural Mountains

R. Yenisey

R. Ob

R. Kolyma

Baltic Sea

R. Volga

Lake Baikal

Sea of Okhotsk

A S I A

Black Sea

Caucasus Mountains

Caspian Sea

Aral Sea

Tien Shan

Kunlun Shan

R. Amur

Gobi Desert

PACIFIC OCEAN

Mediterranean Sea

Plateau of Tibet

Himalaya Mountains

R. Yangtze

R. Indus

R. Ganges

AFRICA

R. Nile

Arabian Sea

Bay of Bengal

South China Sea

Ethiopian Highlands

R. Congo

Lake Victoria

EQUATOR

Lake Tanganyika

Lake Nyasa

INDIAN OCEAN

R. Zambezi

Kalahari Desert

R. Limpopo

AUSTRALIA

Great Dividing Range

R. Darling

ANTARCTICA

Unit 11: Egypt

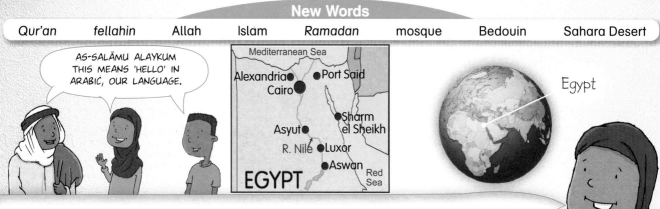

Egypt

Hi, my name is Jamila and I live in Egypt, Africa. Look at the large map of Egypt on page 53.

My Home

My brother and I live with our parents in a small village beside the River Nile. My grandfather says our ancestors helped to build the pyramids for the Pharaohs. I never built a pyramid, but I did help my father to build our house. We collected mud from the banks of the Nile and made it into bricks. We laid them out in the sun until they were baked. It's very hot in Egypt, but the thick walls of our house help to keep it cool inside. We sometimes paint parts of our houses blue to protect us from bad luck. When it gets too hot inside, we sleep on the flat roof. When my brother gets married, he will build another room on the roof for his family. You might think it's strange that we do not have running water or electricity, but I love my house.

My house

Farming

Most members of my family have been farmers or *fellahin*. Much of Egypt is desert, but the land beside the Nile is good for growing crops. We grow beans, wheat and corn, but we can't make a living from farming, so my father works in a factory in the city. When he's away, my brother is in charge of the farm. He can be very bossy. Are all brothers like that? While he uses a water buffalo to plough the fields, I collect water from the well in a large clay jar. I carry it on my head and never spill a drop! I also look after the animals. I milk the water buffalo and goats and I collect their dung for fuel for our fire. Yuck! We also keep pigeons in a tall mud dovecote. I have to collect their droppings too, to spread on the land to help the crops to grow. That's another stinky job, but I don't mind because the pigeons lay delicious eggs. On special occasions we have roasted pigeon stuffed with rice. Yummy! What's your favourite food?

Two dovecotes

Subject:	Geography	Strand:	Human Environments
Strand Unit:	People and Other Lands		

Food

Instead of knives and forks, we use bread called *aysh* to scoop up our food. The women in our village bake *aysh* in clay ovens. They sometimes make *aysh shams* (sun-bread), which are left out in the sun to bake. Our bread is flat like pitta bread.

Aysh shams

One of the things we eat a lot of is *fuul*. It is made with stewed beans, oil, lemon and spices. We only eat meat on special occasions, but never pork. We are Muslims and our religion, Islam, doesn't allow us to eat pork. We only eat *halal*. These are foods that are allowed by our holy book, the *Qur'an*. Meat has to be prepared in a special way according to the instructions in the *Qur'an*. For example, the butcher must call out God's name, Allah, when killing an animal.

Dried fruit

Here is a delicious Egyptian dessert called *khoshaf* for you to make at home or in school: Put 1 cup of dried prunes, 1 cup of dried apricots, 1 cup of dried figs (halved) and $1\frac{1}{2}$ cups of raisins in a container. Sprinkle 1 cup of sugar on top. Pour $2\frac{1}{2}$ cups of boiling water over the top and cover. When the fruit has cooled down, put it in the fridge and serve the next day.

Clothes

Fellahin men wear loose cotton robes in the summer and woollen ones in the winter. These robes are called *jalabiyas*. Some men also wear scarves wound around their heads like turbans. In public, my mother wears a

Gold bracelets

black coat-dress over her brightly-coloured house dress. Her hair is covered with a long scarf and she wears lots of silver and gold necklaces, bracelets and anklets that her parents gave to her when she got married. She says that this is her wealth in case my father dies.

Activities

1. Name five Egyptian cities built on the River Nile.

2. Explain what these Arabic words mean: **(a)** *As-Salāmu Alaykum* **(b)** *fellahin*, **(c)** *aysh shams*, **(d)** *fuul*, **(e)** *Qur'an*, **(f)** *jalabiyas*, **(g)** *khoshaf*, **(h)** *halal*

3. Make a list of five ways in which your life is different to Jamila's and five ways in which it is the same.

4. Design a menu for an Egyptian restaurant, including some of the foods mentioned by Jamila.

5. Write three reasons why Jamila's family keep pigeons.

6. Draw a picture of a *fellahin* man and woman. Label their clothes.

My name is Karim and I am nine years old. I live in an apartment with my family in Cairo, the capital of Egypt.

My Home

Cairo is a busy city, full of traffic, shops, restaurants and tourists. Millions of tourists come to my country each year to see the Great Pyramid at Giza, one of the Seven Wonders of the Ancient World. The unit of currency in Egypt is called the Egyptian pound and it is divided into 100 piastres.

School

Every morning at assembly, we sing the national anthem and salute the Egyptian flag. In class, I study many of the same subjects as you, but not Gaeilge. The subject I find most difficult is English, because the alphabet is so different to Arabic letters and I'll never get used to reading from left to right on a page. In Arabic, we read and write from right to left. When we open a book, we start at what you would call the last page. There are 18 letters in Arabic writing, but you can put a dot above or below some of the letters to make an extra 10 letters.

Games

I am good at soccer and I support the Al-Ahly soccer team, which plays in Cairo Stadium. They would beat Manchester United any day! I also play basketball, video games and a board game called Seega. You can learn how to make and play this game in your Activity Book.

Islam

Like most Egyptians, I'm a Muslim. My religion is Islam and it's very important to me. I study the *Qur'an* and every Friday, I go to the mosque to pray. *Ramadan* is the holiest month of the year, when Muslims do not eat or drink from sunrise to sunset. We eat before dawn and then again after sunset. At the end of *Ramadan*, there's a three-day celebration called *Eid ul-Fitr*. It's my favourite time of the year. Houses are decorated, schools are closed and children receive presents just as you do at Christmas.

Egyptian flag

Hot Geography

Egypt is one of only three countries in the world (the others are Turkey and Russia) that lies in two continents. Part of it is in Asia and part is in Africa!

Seega

A mosque in Cairo

Subject:	Geography	Strand:	Human Environments
Strand Unit:	People and Other Lands		

My name is Zayed and I'm part of a Bedouin tribe that lives in the deserts of Egypt.

The Bedouin

We are nomadic people. That means we are always on the move, searching for water and grazing land for our animals. We travel in large family groups with a leader called a *sheik*. We live in wool tents that are rolled up and carried on camels' backs. Our long robes protect us from the sun and the cloths around our heads keep the sand out of our faces.

Deserts

'Bedouin' means 'people of the desert'. Almost all of Egypt is covered in desert. It gets extremely hot and very few plants, animals or people can survive there. After thousands of years here, Bedouin people know everything about the desert. We can tell from tracks in the sand what direction other travellers have taken. We can tell what animals they had and even the age of their camels! By looking at desert plants, we can tell when it last rained and how much rain fell. We never get lost in the desert, because we navigate by looking at the stars and using markers left on previous trips. Sometimes we leave stores of food or water hanging in trees. Other travellers are welcome to eat and drink from those stores.

Desert Animals

Fennec fox

The fennec fox is suited to desert life because its huge ears give off heat like radiators, helping it to keep cool. It rests in its burrow by day and hunts at night, when it is cooler. Camels are also suited to living in the desert. They can cope with the scorching heat, have long eyelashes to keep sand out of their eyes and can travel for days without water. We use camels to transport goods across the desert. This is why they are known as the 'ships of the desert'. A thirsty camel can drink 100 litres of water in just 10 minutes!

Camels

Hot Geography

Part of the biggest desert in the world is in Egypt. The Sahara Desert gets no more than 10 centimetres of rain a year and temperatures reach over 50 °C.

Hot Geography

You can tell by a Bedouin woman's headgear if she is single or married. Blue headgear means she is not married and red means that she is.

The River Nile in Ancient Egypt

The one thing that connects Jamila, Karim and Zayed is the River Nile. It also connects us with Egypt's ancient history. Every spring in Ancient Egypt, the Nile would flood. When the flood waters went back, a black, rich, fertile soil was left behind, in which farmers could grow crops. The Ancient Egyptians called this the 'gift of the Nile'. The river also gave them other gifts, too. It gave them clean water to drink and bathe in, as well as providing a way to transport goods. It is not surprising that most of Egypt's ancient monuments and cities are found on the banks of the Nile.

The River Nile

At 6650 kilometres long, the Nile is the longest river in the world. It flows into the Mediterranean Sea at the Nile Delta, a large area of fertile soil that has been farmed for thousands of years. Half of the population of Egypt lives around the Nile Delta. Without the Nile, Egypt would be just a desert. Water levels in the river often changed. Sometimes in the past, floods wiped out crops. Other years, the levels were so low that there was drought and famine. The Aswan Dam was built to control the water levels of the Nile.

Another 'gift of the Nile' was the papyrus plant. Ancient Egyptians used the plant to make baskets, sandals, mats, rope and paper!

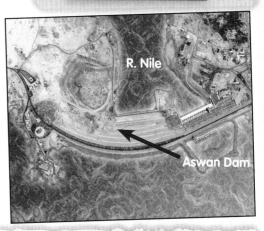

R. Nile

Aswan Dam

Activities

A. Can You Remember?

1. What does Jamila use to eat instead of a knife and fork?
2. What is the leader of a Bedouin tribe called?
3. What is the largest desert in the world?

B. Fill in the Blanks.

Most people in Egypt are Muslim. Their religion is called _____. They go to the mosque on _____ and their holy book is the _____. They go to a _____ to pray. Muslims are not allowed to eat _____. They can only eat _____, which are foods allowed by the *Qur'an*. During _____, Muslims do not eat or drink from _____ until _____. When _____ is over, they have a celebration called _____. It lasts for _____ days.

Subject: Geography **Strand:** Human Environments
Strand Unit: People and Other Lands

Unit 12: Rainforests

New Words

equator   tropical   canopy   extinct   endanger   humid   decomposition   nutrients   tree felling

HELLO, I'M TOCO THE TOUCAN. WELCOME TO MY WORLD. I LIVE IN A COUNTRY CALLED BRAZIL, IN A SPECIAL AREA CALLED THE RAINFOREST. THE RAINFOREST IS AN AMAZING PLACE, WITH LOTS OF DIFFERENT TYPES OF ANIMALS AND PLANTS.

Amazon Rainforest, Brazil

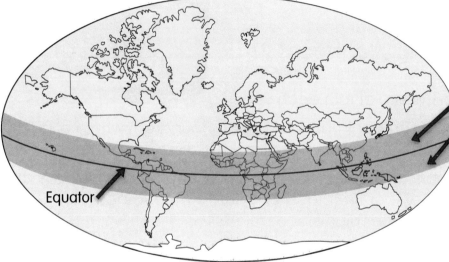

Tropical zones

Equator

Hot Geography

The equator is an imaginary line around the Earth, half-way between the North and South Poles.

Where Are Rainforests Found?

Rainforests are found in tropical zones. Tropical zones are found above and below the equator. In those areas, the sun is very strong during the day and it shines almost every day of the year. That means that rainforests have a tropical climate. Although rainforests are very warm, they also have lots of rain. Some of the world's rainforests get up to 3 centimetres of rain each day of the year. Rainforests are found in a number of countries in the continents of North and South America, Africa, Asia and Australia. The largest rainforest in the world is the Amazon Rainforest in South America. Although rainforests cover only a small area of the Earth's surface, they contain more than half of the Earth's plants and animals.

Brazil

Amazon Rainforest

Subject:	Geography	Strand:	Environmental Awareness and Care
Strand Unit:	Environmental Awareness		

Subject:	Science	Strand:	Environmental Awareness and Care
Strand Unit:	Environmental Awareness		

Hot Geography

An area of rainforest the size of a football field is being destroyed every second.

Rainforest Features

Tropical rainforests have millions of different types of plants and animals. There are so many that scientists believe that they have not all been discovered yet. The tall trees in the rainforest stay green throughout the year. Palm trees are the most common type of tree in the rainforest. Some rainforest trees and plants are used for medicine. In fact, more than one-quarter of all the medicines in the world come from rainforest trees and plants.

Palm trees

All rainforests are different, but the following features are common to all.

- All rainforests lie in tropical areas.

- All rainforests have a canopy. The canopy is the top layer of leaves on all the trees. In the rainforest, it is like a leafy roof!

- Rainforests get more than 1 metre of rain each year.

Rainforest canopy

- Rainforests have lots of plants and animals that are not found anywhere else in the world. More than 50 million different types of animal are found in them.

- The plants and animals of the rainforest depend on one another, as they are all members of a food chain. If one of the plants or animals were to become extinct, it would endanger the lives of other plants and animals.

The Rainforest Floor

Insects and small reptiles live on the forest floor. There may also be larger animals like elephants and jaguars. The rainforest floor is shady and humid (the air has lots of moisture). These conditions play a very important part in the life of the rainforest. A process called decomposition takes place on the forest floor. This happens when dead plants and animals rot. As they rot, or decompose, their remains provide nutrients, or food, to the soil.

Activities

1. Where are rainforests found?
2. Are rainforests warm and dry throughout the year?
3. How do some of the plants of the rainforest help us?
4. Name four countries along the equator.
5. List four features that are common to all rainforests.

Rainforest floor

Subject:	Geography	Strand:	Environmental Awareness and Care
Strand Unit:	Environmental Awareness		

Subject:	Science	Strand:	Environmental Awareness and Care
Strand Unit:	Environmental Awareness		

Rainforest Animals

In the rainforest, most animals live up high in the trees in the canopy. The rainforest floor is warm, dark and damp. Not many animals like those conditions. The canopy can be up to 30 metres above the ground and it is made up of overlapping branches and leaves. The canopy is so thick, or dense, that it blocks most of the sunlight from reaching the rainforest floor. The canopy is the home, or habitat, of many animals such as monkeys, lizards, sloths, jaguars, frogs, and brightly-coloured birds. During the day, the canopy is drier and hotter than any other part of the rainforest. Many animals stay there during the day, calling out to each other and swinging from tree to tree.

Black-and-white colobus

Black-and-white Colobus

What a grumpy face! The black-and-white colobus monkey lives in the rainforests of Africa. It is one of Africa's 10 most endangered animals. It lives high up in the canopy and it eats mostly leaves. It lives in a group called a troop. The members of the troop all look out for one another. They are famous for jumping from tree to tree.

Emerald Tree Boa

This snake lives in the Amazon Rainforest. By day, it curls up asleep in the canopy, but by night, it is a deadly killer. The boa travels quickly through the treetops, searching for its dinner. Once it finds some tasty prey such as a lizard, it wraps its body around it and squeezes it tightly until it is dead. It then swallows it head firsssssst!

Emerald tree boa

Macaw

The macaw is a beautiful, brightly-coloured member of the parrot family. Macaws are found in all of the rainforests of Central and South America. They have large, powerful beaks that they use to crack nuts. Their scaly tongues have a bone that helps them tap into hard fruits such as coconuts. Macaws are very clever birds and have been known to copy human speech.

Macaw

Tribal Indian homes

People of the Rainforests

People have lived in the rainforests for thousands of years. They are called tribal Indians. They survive on plants and animals by hunting, gathering and fishing. They also make medicines from what they find in the rainforest. Their

Tribal Indian home

houses are made from logs covered with grass and palm leaves. If the ground is swampy, they build their houses on stilts. In some places, people live together in small villages.

As the rainforest is hot and humid, the Indian people wear little or no clothing. They often paint their bodies and wear colourful jewellery and headdresses made from beautiful feathers. We can learn a lot from the people who live in the rainforests. They are experts at making medicine from plants and they understand and respect how the plants and animals of the rainforest work together. Unfortunately, many Indian people have lost their homes, as companies have destroyed parts of the rainforest to create land for rearing cattle and growing crops.

Tribal Indians of the Amazon Rainforest

The Importance of Protecting Rainforests

Millions of people live in the rainforests. Many animals and plants live there and they depend on each other for survival. Animals depend on plants for food and shelter. Plants depend on animals to spread their pollen and seeds and to help them to grow. Many foods such as cocoa beans (from which we make chocolate), nuts and coffee beans come from the rainforests. Rainforests are often called the 'lungs of the planet', because the trees recycle carbon dioxide and release oxygen (which we breathe in) back into the air.

Why Are Rainforests Being Destroyed?

Tropical rainforests grow in some of the world's poorest countries. Every year, an area of rainforest the size of Ireland is cut down.

The animals living there either die or move away. Humans are destroying the rainforest to make money from timber and to create land for farming. Scientists are trying to teach people that the rainforests are very important for our survival on Earth and that they should be left alone.

| Subject: | Geography | Strand: | Environmental Awareness and Care |
| Strand Unit: | Environmental Awareness |

| Subject: | Science | Strand: | Environmental Awareness and Care |
| Strand Unit: | Environmental Awareness |

Tree Felling

Scientists believe that the Earth's temperature is rising. In this century alone, it has risen by 1.5 °C. This may not seem like a lot, but any increase in the Earth's temperature affects weather and climates.

CUTTING DOWN TREES IS CHANGING THE WEATHER IN SOME PARTS OF OUR COUNTRY.

BUT WE NEED MORE ROOM FOR FARMING.

WHEN THE TREES ARE FELLED AND BURNED, THEY RELEASE CARBON DIOXIDE, WHICH RISES INTO THE AIR AND CREATES A BLANKET AROUND THE EARTH. THIS KEEPS THE HEAT IN AND RAISES THE TEMPERATURE.

Tree felling in the Amazon Rainforest

What You Can Do to Help

- Look out for the Rainforest Alliance symbol when you are buying food. It means that the food you are buying was produced on farms that are environmentally friendly.

- Stop waste! Use less paper and don't forget to reduce, re-use and recycle. Use both sides of your sheet of paper, because paper is made from trees.

- Ask your teacher if the school is using environmentally friendly paper.

- Tell others about the importance of saving the rainforests.

Activities

A. Answer the Questions.

1. Describe the canopy and the animals that are found there.
2. Why are rainforests important for the Earth?
3. List three foods that we eat that come from the rainforests.
4. List four things that you can do to help stop the destruction of rainforests.
5. List three new things that you learned about life in the rainforests.

B. Find the Mistake in Each Sentence. Write the Sentence Correctly.

1. A small amount of the medicines in the world come from the rainforests.
2. Rainforests are home to animals only.
3. People of the rainforests wear warm hats and coats during the day.
4. The rainforests get bigger and bigger each year.

C. Write Questions for the Following Answers.

1. People in the rainforests live in houses made from logs, grass and palm trees.
2. The animals either die or move away.
3. Tree felling destroys the rainforests and the environment.

Unit 13: Sound

Questions About Sound

What sounds might the children hear in each of the pictures above? How do we use sound to communicate? How do we use sounds to relax or enjoy ourselves? How are sounds used as warnings? Why do animals use sounds?

Sound Travels in Waves

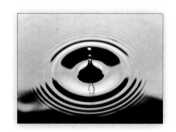

If you were to drop a pebble into a pool of still water, waves would spread outwards from where the pebble hit the water. Sound travels through the air in a similar way; in sound waves. Did you ever shout inside a cave and hear an echo? That happens when the sound waves have nowhere to go. They bounce back off a wall and you hear them again.

Echolocation

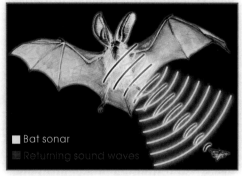

Bat sonar
Returning sound waves

Bats use echolocation to help them to find their way around in the dark. They make sounds that are so high-pitched that a human cannot hear them. When the sound waves hit an object, an echo bounces back. The bat collects the echo with its ears. The bat can tell what the object is by the sound of the echo. Bats can find tiny insects in the dark by using echolocation. Maybe we should stop saying 'as blind as a bat', because bats are not blind. In fact, they can see very well – not only with their eyes, but with their ears too! Some humans have learned echolocation. A blind boy called Ben Underwood, who lived in the USA, discovered echolocation at the age of five. By making clicking noises with his tongue, he was able to find objects, based on the echo that bounced back. He could even tell what those objects were! Using echolocation, he was able to rollerblade, skateboard, ride a bicycle and play football.

Subject:	Science	Strand:	Energy and Forces
Strand Unit:	Sound		

Investigate: How Do Sound Waves Travel?

You will need: A bowl, cling film, baking tray, wooden spoon, sugar

Method:

1. Stretch the cling film tightly over the bowl.

2. Sprinkle a small amount of sugar onto the cling film.

3. Hold the baking tray above the sugar and hit the tray with the wooden spoon. The sound makes the air vibrate and when the sound waves reach the cling film, they make it vibrate. This makes the sugar dance.

Tests:

- Try holding the baking tray further away from the sugar. What happens?

- Try it with other noises. Can you make the sugar dance by shouting?

The Ear

Sound waves are caused by a moving object making the air vibrate. Sound waves travel to your eardrum and make it vibrate, just as the sound waves made the cling film vibrate in the experiment above. When the eardrum vibrates, it makes a tiny bone called the hammer, hit another tiny bone called the anvil. That vibration is sent to your brain as an electrical signal. The brain recognises that signal as a sound.

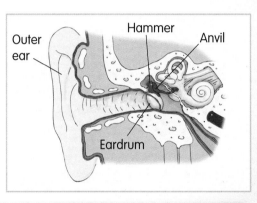

IS THAT WHY PEOPLE DO THIS WHEN THEY FIND IT HARD TO HEAR SOMETHING? ARE THEY TRYING TO COLLECT MORE SOUND WAVES WITH THEIR HAND?

YES. YOUR EAR IS SHAPED LIKE A DISH TO COLLECT SOUND WAVES, JUST LIKE A SATELLITE DISH COLLECTS TELEVISION SIGNALS. PUTTING YOUR HAND TO YOUR EAR HELPS YOU TO COLLECT MORE SOUND WAVES. PEOPLE ALSO PUT THEIR HANDS TO THEIR MOUTH TO MAKE THEIR VOICE LOUDER.

Investigate: How Do Sound Waves Travel?

You will need: Two sheets of thin card, scissors, sticky tape

Method:

1. Roll the sheets of card into cone shapes and tape them so they do not unroll. Trim the edges to make the ends even.

2. Walk away from a friend until you can barely hear each other talking.

3. Now speak into the loud-speaker and tell your friend to listen with the ear trumpet. Does it make a difference? Can you hear each other better?

How to Be a Spy!

You can hear what a person is saying through a closed door. Hold the rim of a glass to the closed door. Put your ear to the bottom of the glass and listen!

Activities

A. Fill in the Blanks.

Sound is caused by a moving object making the air vibrate. The vibrations are called _____ waves. The waves travel into our ears and make our _____ vibrate. This makes a tiny bone called the _____ strike another tiny bone called the _____. Those vibrations are sent to our _____ as an electrical signal.
You can improve your hearing by using an ear _____.
It was used before the hearing aid was invented. You can use a _____ to hear through a closed door.

B. Draw.

Draw or trace a diagram of the ear and label it. You could also show sound waves going into the ear.

Facts About Hearing

Earwax protects your ear. While it is okay to wash the opening of your ear, you should never put anything inside your ear to clean it. Even a cotton bud could seriously damage your ear if you push it too far into your ear.

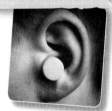

Earplug

Noisy machines, loud music and other loud noises can damage your hearing and cause hearing loss. Always wear earplugs if you are near loud machines and never listen to loud music – especially not with headphones. Turn down the volume!

The loudness of sound is measured in decibels or dB, named after Alexander Graham Bell, who invented the telephone. Listening to any sound over 90 decibels for a long time could damage your hearing.

Your ears affect your balance. Did you ever wonder why you get dizzy after spinning around? Liquid, or fluid, in your ears tells your brain when you are moving. When you spin, the fluid in your ears moves. When you stop spinning, the fluid in your ears keeps moving for a while. A message goes to your brain saying that you are still moving, even though you are not. That is why you feel dizzy.

Spinning on a roundabout

Hot Science

Arulanantham Suresh Joachim holds the world record for balancing on one foot. He balanced on one foot for 76 hours and 40 minutes (more than three days!).

Subject:	Science	Strand:	Energy and Forces
Strand Unit:	Sound		

Feeling Vibrations

People who are deaf cannot hear sounds, but they can still feel vibrations. Evelyn Glennie is a world-famous drummer who is also deaf. She makes music by feeling the vibrations made by her instruments. People who are deaf can also dance by feeling the vibrations of music. Deaf people can talk to each other with sign language. Can you spell your name in sign language?

Evelyn Glennie

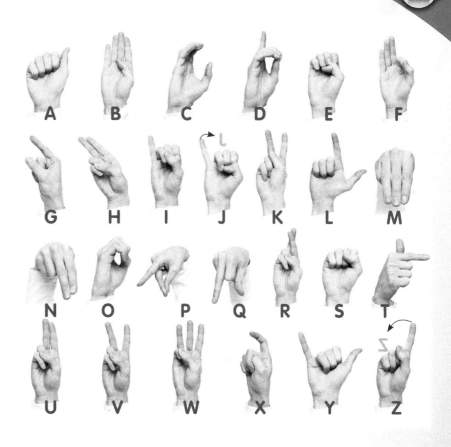

Sign language alphabet

 Design and Make: Your Own Musical Instruments

A. You will need: Eight glass bottles or jam jars (all the same size), water, a long nail

Make a bottle or jam jar organ.

1. Pour a little water into the first bottle. Pour a little more water into the next bottle and so on.
2. Fill the last bottle up to the top with water.
3. Hit the top of each bottle with the nail to make different notes.
4. Try playing 'Three Blind Mice'.

B. You will need: Eight drinking straws, scissors, sticky tape

Make panpipes.

1. Cut eight straws into different lengths.
2. Arrange them from shortest to longest and make sure that they are level at the top.
3. Tape them together with sticky tape.
4. To play the panpipes, blow gently across the top of each straw to make a note.
5. Try playing a tune.

Facts About Sound

The speed of light is faster than the speed of sound: You can see things before you can hear them. Sometimes when a footballer kicks a ball far away from us, we see him or her kick the ball before we hear the thud. During a storm, we always see the lightning before we hear the thunder. To find out how far away a thunderstorm is, count the number of seconds between the flash of lightning and the sound of thunder. Divide your answer by 3 and you will get a good estimate of the distance in kilometres.

Sound needs air to travel: There is no air in space, so there is no sound in space. You would not even hear yourself shout in space. In the picture, the astronaut in the space shuttle can hear the explosion, because there is air in the space shuttle that allows the sound to travel. The other astronaut cannot hear anything because there is no air to carry the sound to her.

Sound travels better through solid objects than through air: Native Americans knew this. By putting their ears to the ground, they could hear the hoof beats of horses long before they heard the sound travelling through the air. Even if you shout, your voice will not travel very far. However, your voice can travel very far on a telephone line. Again, this is because sound travels better through a solid item (a telephone line) than through the air.

Activities

A. Write a 'Sound Fact' for Each of the Following.

1. decibels
2. sign language
3. bats
4. space
5. Native Americans
6. ear trumpet
7. lightning
8. Evelyn Glennie

B. Measure Decibel Levels.

Write the following sounds in order, starting with the quietest:

bird calls, breathing, jet take-off, rustling leaves, motorbike, vacuum cleaner

Sound	Decibel level
	10
	20
	40
	70
	100
Jet take-off	150

C. Digging Deeper.

Use the internet to find out more about Alexander Graham Bell, Evelyn Glennie and Ben Underwood. Write your findings in your copy or do a project.

Subject: Science Strand: Energy and Forces Strand Unit: Sound

Unit 14: The Human Body

New Words

joints   nerves   cartilage   stirrup   femur   calcium   bone marrow   plaster cast   X–ray

ball and socket

Your Skeleton

Your body is always moving, even when you are asleep! You are able to move because of the way that your bones, muscles, joints, nerves and brain all work together. Let's take a closer look at the human body. It is held together and made stronger by parts that we cannot see. Those parts are called bones. Without bones, our bodies would flop about like jelly on a plate! When you were born, you had about 300 bones. As you grow, some of your bones join together, until you finally have 206 bones as an adult. Bones come in all shapes and sizes: long, short, flat, round. Each of your bones has a name. Together they make up the human skeleton.

THINK OF ALL OF THE WAYS THAT YOUR BODY CAN MOVE. IT CAN GO BACKWARDS, FORWARDS, UP AND DOWN. HAVE YOU EVER THOUGHT ABOUT WHAT MAKES YOUR BODY MOVE?

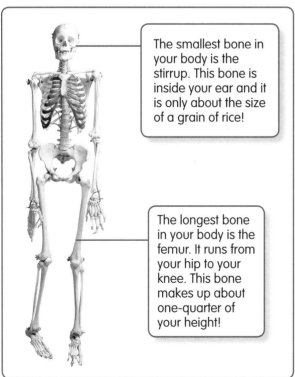

The smallest bone in your body is the stirrup. This bone is inside your ear and it is only about the size of a grain of rice!

The longest bone in your body is the femur. It runs from your hip to your knee. This bone makes up about one-quarter of your height!

Hot Science

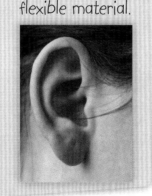

Your nose and ears are not made from bone. They are made from cartilage, which is a strong and flexible material.

Hot Science

Your nose and ears will keep growing all your life!

Your Bones

Your bones are mainly made up of water and a hard material called calcium. The outside of a bone is tough and hard, but the inside is soft and it is made from a spongy type of material. Many bones have bone marrow inside them. Bone marrow looks and feels like jelly and it helps in making new red blood cells, which carry oxygen around your body.

Although your bones are strong and tough, they can sometimes break or snap. Bones are able to heal themselves, but sometimes they need help from a doctor. The doctor may put a plaster cast on a broken bone to make sure that it mends correctly. Hospitals take special photographs, or X-rays, of a bone to see if it is broken.

Bones have lots of different jobs to do. Your skull, backbone and ribcage protect your vital organs. Other bones, such as those in your arms and legs, act as levers.

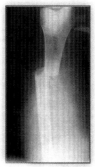
This broken femur will need a plaster cast to mend correctly

The ribs in your chest are like bars in a cage. They help to protect your lungs and heart. If you place your hands on your chest, you should be able to feel the bones that make up your ribcage.

Your skull is a hollow, bony shell that sits on top of your neck. Your skull helps to protect your brain. When you were born, your skull was soft. As you got older, your skull turned into hard bone. The bones in your skull look like a jigsaw that has been pieced together.

Your backbone is a series of bones that runs along the length of your back. Your backbone is also called your spine. It is made up of 33 bones. Your backbone helps to keep you upright and moving. It also protects the nerves that run along your back.

The bones in your arms and legs act like levers. They help you to hold objects, lift, move and run.

Hot History

The first X-ray was taken by Wilhelm Conrad Röntgen in 1895. He took the X-ray of his wife's hand.

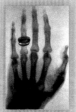

You can see her wedding ring!

Hot Science

Believe it or not, you have a tailbone! You will find it at the very bottom of your spine.

Your Joints

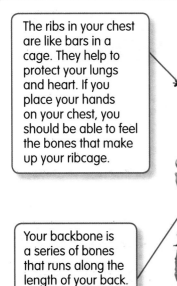
Hinge joint (elbows, knees and fingers)

Ball-and-socket joint (shoulders and hips)

Your bones meet at joints. The joints allow your skeleton to bend and move. Without joints, you would only be able to move your eyebrows and tongue! There are about 100 joints in your body, including your ankles, shoulders, hips, fingers and knees. Joints allow your body to twist, turn and bend in certain ways. The joint in your shoulder is a ball-and-socket joint. It allows you to swing your arms back and forth and sideways. The joint in your elbow works like a hinge, allowing you to move your arm up and down.

Subject:	Science	Strand:	Living Things
Strand Unit:	Human Life		

Activities

A. Answer the Questions.

1. How do joints help your skeleton to move?

2. **(a)** Find two hinge joints and two ball-and-socket joints in your body.
   (b) Why are they located there?

3. Look at the X-rays below. Can you figure out which body part is shown in each one?

(a) 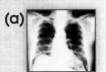 (b) 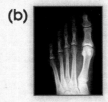 (c)  (d) 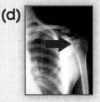 (e)

B. Find the Mistake(s) in Each Sentence. Write the Sentence Correctly.

1. The femur is the smallest bone in your body and it is located in your nose.

2. You had 206 bones when you were born and you will grow more bones as you get older.

3. The joints in your skeleton stop it from moving. Your body has about 10 joints.

More New Words

| carbohydrates | protein | enamel | incisors | canines | premolars | molars | cavities |

Food and Energy

Food gives you energy. It helps your body to keep your heart beating, your lungs breathing and your muscles and joints moving. To have a healthy, balanced diet, we eat fresh fruit, vegetables and meat (or meat alternatives). Try to eat a variety of foods. The food pyramid shows us the types of food that we need for healthy bodies and minds. Bread, pasta and rice have carbohydrates, which give our bodies energy. Fresh fruit and vegetables have vitamins, which we need for healthy muscles and skin and to fight infection. Milk, cheese and yoghurt have calcium, which we need for healthy bones. Meat, fish and eggs give us the protein that we need for growth and repair of cells. Fried or sugary foods give us fat. We should avoid those foods.

Food pyramid

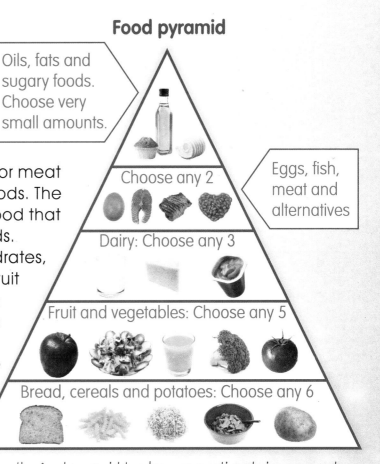

Oils, fats and sugary foods. Choose very small amounts.

Choose any 2

Eggs, fish, meat and alternatives

Dairy: Choose any 3

Fruit and vegetables: Choose any 5

Bread, cereals and potatoes: Choose any 6

Use the food pyramid to plan your portion choices every day

| Subject: | Science | Strand: | Living Things |
| Strand Unit: | Human Life | | |

Traffic Light Plan

Remember: For a healthy lifestyle, try to follow the traffic light plan:

Stop! I should avoid the following foods:
Sweets, crisps, fried food, fizzy drinks

Caution! I should only eat the following foods sometimes:
Dairy products, eggs, white bread, biscuits

Go! The following foods are good to eat:
Fresh fruit and vegetables, wholegrain bread, pasta and rice, lean meat such as chicken or fish, beans, lentils

Your Teeth

Your teeth are very important for breaking down food for your body to digest and absorb. Your teeth are located in your jaws, which are part of your skull. All of your teeth are covered by a white material called enamel. Enamel is one of the toughest materials in your body and it is even stronger than most types of rock! If you rub your finger (make sure it is clean!) along your teeth, you will notice that they are rough and have little bumps or ridges. They help your teeth to bite, gnash, munch, chew and break down your food. There are four main types of teeth: incisors, canines, premolars and molars.

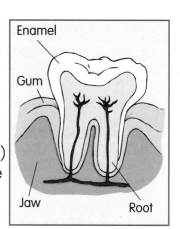

The tooth

NEXT TIME YOUR TOOTH FALLS OUT, LOOK AT IT CAREFULLY BEFORE YOU LEAVE IT FOR THE TOOTH FAIRY.

Children have 20 teeth in a set. These 'baby' teeth all start to fall out at around age six and adult teeth begin to grow. There are 32 teeth in an adult set.

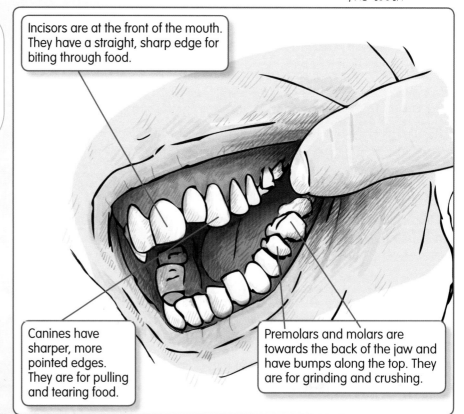

Incisors are at the front of the mouth. They have a straight, sharp edge for biting through food.

Canines have sharper, more pointed edges. They are for pulling and tearing food.

Premolars and molars are towards the back of the jaw and have bumps along the top. They are for grinding and crushing.

Subject:	Science	Strand:	Living Things
Strand Unit:	Human Life		

Taking Care of Your Teeth

Your teeth are strong and tough, but like your body, they need to be looked after. Strong, healthy teeth help you to chew your food. They also help you to speak clearly. You should clean your teeth properly by brushing them at least twice a day. Otherwise, germs may build up in your mouth and cause little holes to form in the enamel. These holes are called cavities. Avoid sugary foods and go to the dentist regularly for check-ups. After all, it is much easier to take care of your teeth than to suffer with a toothache!

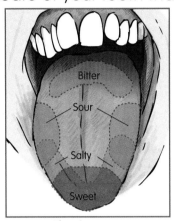

The tongue

Hot History

Toothpaste was invented only 100 years ago. Before that, people used ashes, chalk, lemon juice and tobacco to clean their teeth!

Your Tongue

Your tongue is a muscle. It moves more than any other muscle in your body. It is covered with more than 10,000 taste buds that help you to identify taste. Each taste bud is actually shaped like an onion! Most of your taste buds are along the top and sides of your tongue. Each section of your tongue identifies a different taste. The tongue can identify sweet, salty, sour and bitter tastes.

Activities

A. Answer the Questions.

1. Why do our bodies need food?

2. What do we mean by a 'balanced diet'?

3. Explain why your body needs each of the following types of food:
   (a) pasta, (b) vegetables, (c) milk, (d) fish

4. Why do you think your body needs more fruit and vegetables than crisps and chocolate?

B. Write Questions for the Following Answers.

1. Teeth are covered by enamel.

2. Enamel is stronger than most types of rock.

3. The canines are located at the front of the mouth and used for pulling and tearing food.

4. People used ash, lemon juice and tobacco to clean their teeth.

5. Little holes in the enamel are called cavities.

C. Explain Each of the Following Words and Phrases.

1. incisors, 2. food pyramid, 3. baby teeth, 4. cavities, 5. carbohydrates

D. Draw.

Draw the food pyramid and label the food groups.

Unit 15: Electricity

New Words

mains   current   fossil fuels   power station   turbines   solar cells   geothermal   pylons   batteries   volts
circuit   terminals   switch   conductors   insulators

IMAGINE IF WE DIDN'T HAVE ELECTRICITY.

YEAH, WE'D HAVE TO WATCH TV BY CANDLELIGHT.

WARNING

All of the activities in this unit require small batteries, which contain very little electricity. Never, ever experiment with mains electricity. It is very dangerous and it can even kill.

How Electricity Is Made

About 100 years ago, few people had electricity in their homes. Now it is hard to imagine life without it. Think about all of the electrical things that you used this morning in your house. Now look around your classroom. How many electrical things can you see? The electricity we use at home and in school is called mains electricity. It is made in a power station. Some power stations burn fossil fuels like gas, coal and peat to make electricity. However, this causes a lot of pollution. Another problem with fossil fuels is that they are running out. Luckily, there are other ways to make electricity.

At Ardnacrusha in County Clare, the power of the River Shannon is used to make electricity.

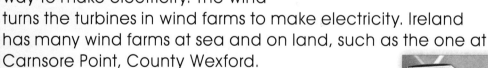

Ardnacrusha

Wind farm

Wind power is another clean way to make electricity. The wind turns the turbines in wind farms to make electricity. Ireland has many wind farms at sea and on land, such as the one at Carnsore Point, County Wexford.

The energy of the sun can also be used to make electricity. Solar cells change sunlight into electricity. You might have seen solar cells on calculators, garden lights, parking meters and road signs. Some houses have solar panels on their roofs.

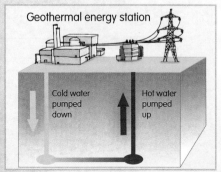

Geothermal energy station

Cold water pumped down

Hot water pumped up

Solar cell

Geothermal energy is made by taking heat from the ground and turning it into electricity. Almost one-third of the electricity created in Iceland is made in this way. Some houses in Ireland have geothermal heating systems.

Subject:	Science	Strand:	Energy and Forces
Strand Unit:	Magnetism and Electricity		

Subject:	Geography	Strand:	Human Environments
Strand Unit:	People Living and Working in the Local Area		

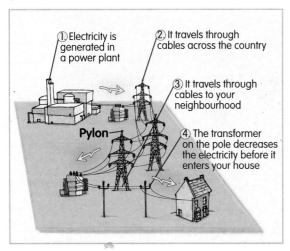

Pylon

① Electricity is generated in a power plant
② It travels through cables across the country
③ It travels through cables to your neighbourhood
④ The transformer on the pole decreases the electricity before it enters your house

How Electricity Gets to Your House

The mains electricity flows from the power station to your house through cables that hang from large towers called pylons. The electricity flows through the cables in much the same way as water flows through pipes. That flow is called an electric current. Once the electricity arrives at your house, it flows through wires into the light switches and sockets. You can then connect electrical machines to the sockets using plugs with metal pins.

Batteries

Mains electricity is not the only type of electricity. We can also get electricity from batteries. Can you think of anything that uses batteries? Batteries are filled with chemicals that make a small amount of electricity. The strength of a battery is measured in volts. The more volts a battery has, the greater power it has. Watches and calculators use tiny batteries, but cars use really big batteries. Can you tell which batteries on the right are watch batteries and which is a car battery? Every battery has a positive (+) and a negative (–) terminal (end). To make electricity flow, the terminals need to be joined together in a circuit.

Investigate: How Does a Circuit Work?

You will need: A small round battery (AA or C), a small torch bulb in a holder, two wires

Method:
1. Set up the circuit as shown, to light the bulb.
2. Electricity can only flow in a circuit.

Tests:
• What happens when you break the circuit?
• What happens if you turn the battery around?
• What would happen if you left the circuit connected for a long time?

Switches

Switches are used to turn on and off electricity. To turn off the electricity, a switch breaks the circuit. To turn on the electricity, a switch joins up the circuit. How many types of switch can you think of?

| Subject: | Science | Strand: | Energy and Forces | Subject: | Geography | Strand: | Human Environments |
| Strand Unit: | Magnetism and Electricity | | | Strand Unit: | People Living and Working in the Local Area | | |

89

Investigate: How Does a Switch Work?

You will need: A simple circuit (see page 89), a piece of wire, corrugated cardboard, two paper fasteners, a paper clip

Method:

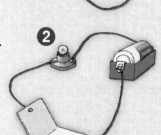

1. Cut out a rectangle of card and fold it in half. Fix the paper fasteners to the card as shown in picture 1. Make sure the paper fasteners touch when the card is folded. This will be the switch.

2. Wrap one end of the piece of wire around one paper fastener. Join the switch to your circuit as shown in picture 2.

3. When the switch is closed, the circuit is complete, and the bulb lights up. When the switch is open, the circuit is broken, and the bulb does not light up.

Test:

- Try making other switches like the one with a paper clip as shown in picture 3.

Activities

1. Make a list of 10 battery-powered or electrical objects that have a switch.
2. Draw a diagram of a circuit and label it.
3. Draw a diagram to show how electricity comes to your house.

Conductors

Electricity can flow through some materials, but not others. Materials through which electricity can flow are called conductors. Metals are good conductors of electricity. That is why copper is used to make electrical wire. Silver and gold are even better conductors of electricity. Why do you think they are not used to make electrical wire?

YOU MEAN LIKE THIS GUY?

NO, HE'S A CONDUCTOR OF MUSIC! WE'RE TALKING ABOUT CONDUCTORS OF ELECTRICITY.

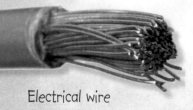

Electrical wire

Insulators

Materials that do not allow electricity to pass through them are called insulators. Plastic is a good insulator. Why do you think electrical wires are coated in plastic?

Subject:	Science	Strand:	Energy and Forces
Strand Unit:	Magnetism and Electricity		

Subject:	Geography	Strand:	Human Environments
Strand Unit:	People Living and Working in the Local Area		

Investigate: Are Materials Conductors or Insulators of Electricity?

You will need: A simple circuit (see page 89), a piece of wire, wood, glass, coin, key, paper clip, crayon, plastic, rubber, paper, drink can, silk, fruit

Method:

1. Set up the simple circuit with three wires, like you did in the switch investigation (page 90). Instead of adding the switch, leave a gap between the two wires.

2. Place the material to be tested in the gap and attach the two wires to it. If the material is a conductor, electricity will pass through it and the bulb will light up. If the material is an insulator, electricity will not pass through it and the bulb will not light up.

3. Before you test each item, guess if it is a conductor or insulator of electricity.

4. Record the results on the record sheet in your Activity Book.

Static Electricity

Did you ever reach out to touch something such as a doorknob and … *ZAP!* … you got a shock? This is because of a type of electricity called static electricity, which does not flow through a wire. It is made when things rub against each other and create a charge. A thunderstorm is caused by static electricity. Inside a storm cloud, pieces of ice rub against each other. The cloud becomes charged, creating a flash of lightning. Many tall buildings such as churches have a metal rod on the roof, called a lightning conductor. It is connected to the ground by a strip of metal. If lightning strikes, the conductor will carry the charge harmlessly into the ground.

Hot History

Lightning strikes Earth more than 100 times per second. Each year, 24,000 people are killed by lightning strikes, but many people also survive. US National Park Ranger, Roy Sullivan, holds a world record for being struck by lightning seven times.

Investigate: How Does Static Electricity Work?

You will need: A balloon, a plate, paper, a woollen jumper

Method:

1. Tear the paper into tiny bits or use a hole-punch.

2. Place the pieces of paper on a plate.

3. Blow up a balloon and rub it against the woollen jumper for a few seconds to make static electricity. Your balloon is now charged.

4. Hold the charged balloon high above the bits of paper.

5. Slowly lower the balloon towards them. What happens?

Test:

- Try holding the balloon over each of the following: a plate of rice crispies; a plate of tiny bits of Styrofoam; a plate of tiny bits of tinfoil. Which works best?

How to Use Electricity Safely

Never leave electrical items on when you are going to bed. Never change light bulbs yourself. Never stick anything into the holes of a socket. Always keep drinks away from electrical items. Do not let leads from electrical items trail across the floor.

Never put lit candles on top of electrical items. Never put too many plugs in a socket; it could cause a fire.

Water and electricity are very dangerous together. Never bring electrical items into the bathroom. Never touch electrical items with wet hands.

Never put items into the microwave oven or washing machine without a grown-up's permission. Never have electrical cables near a cooker. Never stick anything into a toaster, even if your toast is stuck. Be careful if an iron is plugged in.

Never play near pylons or electricity stations. Never touch the bare metal in electrical wires.

Activities

A. Answer the Questions.

1. What type of electricity does not flow through wires?
2. What do you call a tower used for holding up electrical cables?
3. What do you call something that does not allow electricity to pass through it?
4. What do you call something used to break and join a circuit?
5. Why should you not bring electrical items into your bathroom?

B. Fill in the Blanks.

Lightning is caused by static _____. When pieces of _____ rub together inside a storm cloud, the cloud becomes charged. The charge is released as a flash of lightning. Lightning hits the Earth _____ times every second. Every year, _____ people die from lightning strikes. Roy _____, a US National Park Ranger, was struck by lightning _____ times. Many tall buildings have a lightning _____ to protect them from lightning.

C. Get Creative.

1. How many things in a car can you name that are powered by electricity? (For example, windscreen wipers.)
2. Choose a piece of electrical safety advice and make a poster about it.

Subject:	Science	Strand:	Energy and Forces
Strand Unit:	Magnetism and Electricity		

Subject:	Geography	Strand:	Human Environments
Strand Unit:	People Living and Working in the Local Area		

Unit 16: The Sun

New Words

supernova | galaxy | solar system | hydrogen | helium | winter solstice | eclipse

WHAT DOES THE SUN DO FOR US?

THE SUN GIVES US...

Light   Heat   Food   ... And Lots More!

Hot Geography

Unlike a fire in your fireplace, the sun does not 'go out'. This is because the sun makes its own fuel. Gases like hydrogen and helium mix together in the sun to create massive explosions. These explosions send light and heat to Earth.

How Old is the Sun?

The sun is a star. Stars are born, they live for a while and then they die when they get old. Our sun is about 4.5 billion years old. It is halfway through its life. It is one of the billions of stars that make up the Milky Way Galaxy. A galaxy is a huge collection, or group, of stars. Everything in our solar system was born when a giant star exploded. The explosion is known as a supernova. Gas, ice and dust surrrounded the newly formed sun. The gas, the ice and the sun crashed into one another and joined up to make the planets and moons of our solar system. The sun is the biggest thing in our solar system. 1.3 million Earth-size planets could fit inside the sun!

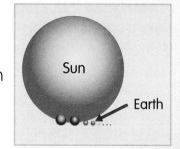

Sun

Earth

Planet Earth Moving and Spinning

It takes the Earth $365\frac{1}{4}$ days (a year) to go around the sun. However, you cannot have one-quarter of a day in a year. Four-quarters make one whole, so every four years, an extra day is added in February. This is called a leap year. While the Earth is moving around the sun, it is also spinning. It takes the Earth 24 hours to do a full spin. This gives us day and night. When it is daytime in Ireland, it is night-time on the other side of the world.

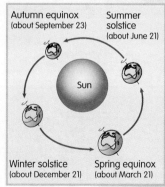

Autumn equinox (about September 23)
Summer solstice (about June 21)
Sun
Winter solstice (about December 21)
Spring equinox (about March 21)

Long and Short Days

A day and a night together make up 24 hours. Days in summer are much longer than days in winter. When we say 'longer' we mean that we have more daylight time in summer than we do in winter. During our winter, the North Pole faces away from the sun. This gives us short days and long nights. Our shortest day of the year, the winter solstice, is around December 21st.

| Subject: | Geography | Strand: | Natural Environments |
| Strand Unit: | Planet Earth in Space | | |

| Subject: | Science | Strand: | Energy and Forces |
| Strand Unit: | Heat | | |

During our summer, the North Pole faces towards the sun. This gives us long days and short nights. Our longest day of the year, the summer solstice, is around June 21st. Day and night at the equator are always of equal length. At the North and South Poles, days last up to 24 hours in summer, while nights last up to 24 hours in winter.

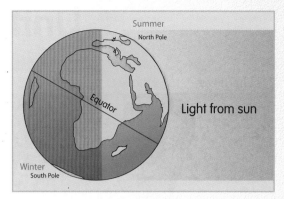

The Solar System

Sometimes scientists change their minds! Long ago, scientists knew that there were six planets: Mercury, Venus, Earth, Mars, Jupiter and Saturn. Then they found another planet (Uranus), then another (Neptune) and then another (Pluto). They made up a way for us to remember the names of the nine planets: *My Very Educated Mother Just Showed Us Nine Planets.* Then they started finding other planets like Sedna and Eris. "Holy Jupiter!" said one scientist. "How will children remember the names of all these planets?" The scientists held a big meeting to decide what to do. "From now on," they said, "there are only eight planets in the solar system. Pluto is too small to be called a planet. It is only a dwarf planet."

Planets of the Solar System

An eclipse occurs when the moon moves between the Earth and the sun. It blocks the light of the sun from reaching Earth.

Mercury is named after the Roman god of travel, because it moves so quickly across the sky. It is a small, rocky planet with no moons.

Venus is named after the Roman god of love and beauty, because it is the brightest planet. It is also the hottest planet.

Earth is the only planet on which there are living things. About three-quarters of its surface is covered with water.

Mars is named after the Roman god of war. It has a mountain that is almost three times taller than Mount Everest. It is called Olympus Mons.

Subject: Geography	**Strand:** Natural Environments
Strand Unit: Planet Earth in Space	

Subject: Science	**Strand:** Energy and Forces
Strand Unit: Heat	

Jupiter is named after the king of the Roman gods. It is the largest planet in our solar system. You could fit 1000 Earth-sized planets inside Jupiter. It is made of gas.

Saturn is the lightest planet and it has 62 moons. Its rings are made from chunks of ice and rock.

Uranus can be seen in the night sky with a telescope. The gas in its atmosphere makes it look blue. It has 27 moons.

Neptune is named after the Roman god of the sea because it is blue. It takes 165 years for Neptune to go around the sun.

Activities

A. Fill in the Blanks.

The sun is about _____ billion years old. It is part of a galaxy called the _____ _____. It was born when a huge star exploded. This is called a _____. It takes the Earth _____ days to move around the sun. The Earth is also spinning. It takes the Earth ____ hours to do a complete spin. That makes day and night. In summer, days are _____, but in winter they are _____.

B. Get Creative.

1. Write clues for the eight planets and ask a friend to fill in the answers. (For example: *I am the largest planet in the solar system. Who am I?*)

2. Make up a new way to remember the eight planets in the solar system. (For example: *Many Very Elderly Monkeys Just Snooze Under Newspapers.*)

More New Words

| opaque | transparent | sundial | carbon dioxide | photosynthesis | • blood vessel | ultraviolet |

siesta

Hot History

The sundial was one of the first clocks. Its symbols stand for times of the day. The sun shines on the pointer and a shadow is cast. The shadow moves as the sun's position in the sky changes.

Shadows and Light

A shadow forms when something is blocking out the light. Things that block the light are described as 'opaque'. You cannot see through opaque items. Buildings, cars and people are opaque. Things like glass, which let light through, are described as 'transparent'. As the Earth spins, the sun seems to move across the sky. The sun rises in the east and sets, or goes down, in the west. As the sun sets, when it is lowest in the sky, it casts the longest shadows. At midday, when the sun is highest in the sky, it casts the shortest shadows.

| **Subject:** | Geography | **Strand:** | Natural Environments |
| **Strand Unit:** | Planet Earth in Space |

| **Subject:** | Science | **Strand:** | Energy and Forces |
| **Strand Unit:** | Heat |

Plants Need the Sun

Plants make their own food by:

1. Taking up water through their roots.

2. Breathing in a gas called carbon dioxide (which we breathe out). They breathe out a gas called oxygen (which we breathe in).

3. Taking in sunlight through tiny holes in their leaves, which it mixes with water and carbon dioxide to make food. This way of making food is called photosynthesis.

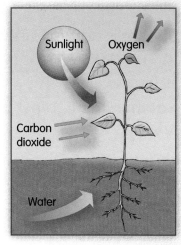

Photosynthesis

Plants Move Towards the Sun

Leaves are flat so that they can catch as much sunlight as possible. Plants will even move towards the light. A sunflower follows the path of the sun from when it rises in the east to when it sets in the west. An indoor pot-plant will lean towards the nearest window. A creeper like ivy will climb a tree or even a house to get closer to the sun. Why do you think the leaves at the top of a tree are smaller than the leaves at the bottom?

Investigate: Do Plants Really Need the Sun?

You will need: Blotting paper, four plates, a glass or jar, bean seeds, a cardboard box

Method:

1. Place damp blotting paper on each of the plates.

2. Sprinkle some bean seeds onto the blotting paper.

3. Put an upturned glass over the first set of seeds.

4. Make a hole in the side of the cardboard box and place it upturned over the second set of seeds.

5. Place the third set of seeds in a cupboard or another dark place.

6. Leave the fourth set of seeds to grow normally.

7. Record the results on the record sheet in your Activity Book.

If you get too cold, your body shivers to warm you up. If you get too hot, your body sweats to cool you down. Cold-blooded creatures, like turtles, cannot do this. They lie in the sun to warm up and hide in the shade to cool down.

Animals and People Need the Sun

Mammals use sunlight to make vitamin D, which helps to make our bones strong. We also breathe deeper and more evenly in the sunshine. Our blood flows better in the sunshine, because our blood vessels, or tubes, open up. People in tropical countries are less likely to have heart attacks than people in colder countries. Scientists think this may be because they get more sunshine.

Subject:	Geography	Strand:	Natural Environments
Strand Unit:	Planet Earth in Space		

Subject:	Science	Strand:	Energy and Forces
Strand Unit:	Heat		

Too Much Sun Can be Dangerous

Too much sunlight can cause the skin to burn (sunburn). It can also dry out the skin and cause wrinkles to form. It can even cause skin cancer. The ultraviolet (UV) rays in sunlight can also damage your eyes. Protect yourself from sunlight by using the information given in the following tips.

- Keep out of the summer sun during the hours around midday, when it is hottest.
- Wear sunscreen to protect your skin from the sun's dangerous UV rays.
- Wear white clothes, as white helps to reflect (throw back) the heat of the sun.
- Wear clothes that fully cover your skin.
- Wear sunglasses to protect your eyes.
- Wear a hat.

People Living in Hot Countries

Spanish house

In hot countries, people are used to coping with the sun. They do not work in the middle of the day, when it is really hot. Often, they have a nap instead. In Spain, this is called a *siesta*. People in hot countries often wear white clothes to reflect the heat of the sun. Their most popular colours for cars are white and silver. Black is not a good colour, because it attracts the heat. Houses often have thick, white walls with small windows to keep out the heat of the sun.

Activities

A. Answer the Questions.

1. What word is used to describe things that block the light?
2. Where does the sun rise and set?
3. What is a sundial?
4. Name the process through which plants make their food.
5. How does your body warm up if it gets too cold?
6. Why is white a popular colour for clothes, cars and houses in hot countries?

B. Get Creative.

1. Draw and label a picture of a plant to show how it gets its food.
2. Design a poster to show people how to protect themselves from the sun.

C. Draw a Graph.

The following table shows the number of moons for each planet. Draw a graph to show the information.

Planet:	Mercury	Venus	Earth	Mars	Jupiter	Saturn	Uranus	Neptune
Moons:	0	0	1	2	16	62	27	8

Mercury

Venus

Earth

Jupiter

Mars

Sun

Mercury is the smallest planet in our solar system and it is closest to the sun. It is an airless, rocky planet. It is very hot on the side facing the sun and freezing cold on the other side. Its surface is covered in craters.

Our planet, Earth, has exactly the right conditions for life as we know it to survive. It is just close enough to the sun to get light and heat. There is oxygen in the atmosphere and a solid surface to stand on. It is the only planet in our solar system with liquid water.

Jupiter is the largest planet in the solar system. It is a giant gas ball with no solid surface. It is extremely cold, with no suitable atmosphere to breathe. Jupiter has a giant storm spot, where hurricanes rage and never seem to end.

Venus is the brightest planet in the sky at night. It is a little smaller than Earth and like Earth, it has a solid surface, continents and mountains. It is the hottest planet and because of toxic gases in its atmosphere, no life could survive there. It is sometimes called the Morning or Evening Star, as we can see it from Earth. A day on Venus lasts for 262 Earth years!

Mars is smaller than Earth. It is known as the 'Red Planet' because of its dusty, red surface. Mars may once have had rivers, lakes and oceans. The atmosphere is thin with traces of oxygen. Mars has two moons.

Uranus

Saturn

Neptune

Pluto

Uranus is several times larger than Earth. It is a giant gas ball that spins on its side. It is also known as an ice giant, as it is so cold. It has 27 moons and 11 invisible rings. Scientists think that there could be a huge ocean and diamonds on the surface of Uranus!

Pluto is called a dwarf planet, or planetoid. It is smaller than Earth's moon. It takes 249 years to travel around the sun. It is a very cold, dark place. Pluto was named after the Roman god of the Underworld by an 11-year-old English girl! (The Roman god Pluto is also known as Hades.)

Saturn is the second largest planet in our solar system. It is also a giant gas ball. It has 62 moons and it takes 29½ years to go around the sun. Saturn has rings of ice, dust and rock. There are huge hurricane storms on Saturn. Saturn is so light that it would float on water!

Neptune is the third largest planet in our solar system. It gets its name from the Roman god of the sea, because the gases in its atmosphere give it a beautiful blue colour. It is also a gas and ice giant. It has a great dark spot caused by a giant storm. It is a very windy planet.

Unit 17: Heat

Have you ever made chocolate rice crispy buns? Try the delicious recipe below, but be careful: there is heat involved. You will need the help of an adult.

Recipe: Chocolate Rice Crispy Buns

You will need: Chocolate, rice crispy cereal, paper bun cases, bowl, spoon to stir, saucepan

Method: Caution: Adult help required!

1. Melt the chocolate in the bowl over a saucepan of hot water.
2. Add the rice crispy cereal and stir until it is evenly mixed.
3. Spoon the mixture into bun cases and allow to cool.

Tip:

- Try adding melted marshmallows and butter, peanut butter or jam to invent your own delicious rice crispy buns!

From Where Does the Heat in Your Home Come?

Heat from the cooker is used to melt the chocolate in the recipe above. A cooker can be powered by electricity or gas. We can also use a microwave oven to heat water. Can you remember how food was cooked long ago? There are many sources of heat in the world today. Some sources of heat are natural and some are unnatural (man-made or artificial).

Natural Forms of Heat

The sun is the natural source of heat on Earth. Without it, all plant and animal life would die.

It is so hot under the surface of the Earth that rocks melt and turn into magma. Magma forces its way to the Earth's surface at a volcano.

There are springs of hot water under the ground. Sometimes a spring gets so hot that it erupts as a geyser.

Many new houses use geothermal heating systems, which take heat from under the ground.

Heat can be made by friction. An example of friction is rubbing your hands together to get warm on a cold day.

| Subject: | Science | Strand: | Energy and Forces / Materials |
| Strand Unit: | Heat (linked to Materials and Change) | | |

| Subject: | Geography | Strand: | Natural Environments |
| Strand Unit: | Weather, Climate and Atmosphere | | |

Heat Can Travel

A good conductor of heat is a material that allows heat to travel easily through it. Metals are good conductors of heat. That is why radiators and saucepans are made from metal. Can you think why the handle of a saucepan is often made from plastic or wood?

Investigate: Which Spoon Should Be Used for Cooking?

You will need: Metal spoon, plastic spoon, wooden spoon, bowl of warm water, butter

Method: Caution: Only adults are allowed to pour hot water!

1. Put a knob of butter at the top of each spoon handle.
2. Place the spoons in the bowl of water.
3. Observe (watch) what happens.

Tests:

- Does the length of the spoon make a difference?
- What else must be kept equal to make the test fair?
- What happens if you use hotter water?

Heat Can Change Things

Materials can be changed into different forms. Some materials can be changed completely by heating. Others can be changed back  to the way they were by cooling. An egg is completely changed by frying and you cannot change it back. Ice will melt into water when it is heated and it will change back to ice again when it is frozen.

Investigate: What Happens When Materials Are Heated?

You will need: Knob of butter, square of chocolate, spoon of sugar, piece of candle wax, four foil containers, desk lamp, a straw

Method:

1. Place the butter, chocolate, sugar and wax into separate foil containers.
2. Place them on a table close to each other but not touching.
3. Switch on the desk lamp. Point it straight down onto the containers, as close as is safely possible (about 5 centimetres away).
4. Observe for about five minutes.
5. Switch off the lamp and stir each material with the straw to see how it has changed.
6. Record the results on the record sheet in your Activity Book.

| Subject: | Science | Strand: | Energy and Forces / Materials |
| Strand Unit: | Heat (linked to Materials and Change) |

| Subject: | Geography | Strand: | Natural Environments |
| Strand Unit: | Weather, Climate and Atmosphere |

101

Activities

A. Answer the Questions.

1. What is the main natural source of heat on our planet?
2. List three sources of heat in your kitchen.
3. List three sources of heat in your classroom.
4. What is a good conductor of heat?
5. What is the name of the melted rock under the surface of the Earth?
6. Where does geothermal heat come from?

B. Think About It.

1. What would happen if we did not have the heat from the sun?
2. Name two things in your kitchen that are designed to protect your hands from burning.
3. Can you think of a country that has a lot of hot springs and geysers?

C. Look Up the Meaning of the Following Words in Your Dictionary.

1. source, 2. conductor, 3. geothermal, 4. friction

Temperature

Look at the label on your clothes. At what temperatures should they be washed? What would happen if the clothes were washed at the wrong temperature? Temperature is a measure of how hot or cold something is. A thermometer is used to measure temperature. We measure temperature using the Celsius scale. The temperature at which water boils is 100 degrees Celsius (100 °C). The temperature at which water freezes is 0 degrees Celsius (0 °C). In the USA, temperature is measured in degrees Fahrenheit (°F).

Thermometers

There are many different types of thermometer, including: medical thermometer; dial thermometer; window thermometer; meat thermometer; car thermometer. For health and safety reasons, there are many times when we need to find an accurate temperature; for example, while cooking meat.

Thermometer scale

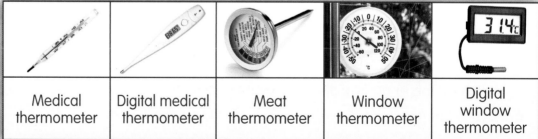

Medical thermometer	Digital medical thermometer	Meat thermometer	Window thermometer	Digital window thermometer

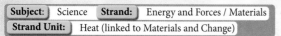

Subject: Science **Strand:** Energy and Forces / Materials
Strand Unit: Heat (linked to Materials and Change)

Subject: Geography **Strand:** Natural Environments
Strand Unit: Weather, Climate and Atmosphere

🔬 Investigate: Which Part of Your Classroom Is Coolest?

You will need: Chocolate buttons, paper plates, thermometers

Method:
1. Place a few chocolate buttons on each plate.
2. Leave the plates in different parts of the classroom, for example, on a sunny windowsill, in a dark press, on/under the radiator, etc. Observe them over a few days to see what happens.

Tests:
- Can you tell by looking at the buttons which place is the warmest?
- Measure the temperature with a thermometer and see if you were right.

Body Temperature

On a hot day, it is important to keep cool, especially if you have been running around a lot! Wearing light clothes will help you to keep cool. Taking a splash in your local pool will also help you to cool down. Mammals and birds are warm-blooded creatures that need to keep a fairly constant temperature inside their bodies. Animals use a variety of methods to warm up when they are cold and to cool down when they get too hot.

Polar bears are mammals. They have black skin under their fur to keep them warm. (Black absorbs heat from the sun.) Polar bears also burrow into the snow to escape the freezing polar winds.	Many mammals such as dogs have thick coats of fur to keep them warm during winter. They shed some of their fur in summer. Dogs pant to cool down, as they lose heat through their tongues.	Large mammals have difficulty cooling down if they get overheated. That is why elephants have large, thin ears, which allow them to lose heat from their bodies quickly.

Crocodiles are cold-blooded creatures. They lie in the sun to get warm. When they want to cool down, they open their mouths wide or laze in the water.	When a cold-blooded reptile such as a snake gets too hot, it will hide away in a shady area, open its mouth wide, lighten its skin colour or burrow into cool soil.	People use fans to cool down. Fanning moves air quickly around the body, helping the sweat on the skin to evaporate. This has a cooling effect.

Subject: Science	**Strand:** Energy and Forces / Materials	**Subject:** Geography	**Strand:** Natural Environments	103
Strand Unit: Heat (linked to Materials and Change)		**Strand Unit:** Weather, Climate and Atmosphere		

Investigate: What Happens When Air Is Heated?

You will need: Balloon, empty plastic bottle, bowl of hot water

Method: Caution: Only adults are allowed to pour hot water!

1. Stretch a balloon over the top of an empty plastic bottle. Observe.
2. Stand the bottle in a bowl of hot water. Observe what happens.

Warm air is lighter than cool air, so warm air rises. A hot air balloon rises because it has a special burner that heats the air inside the balloon.

Design and Make: A Mini Greenhouse

You will need: Seeds (herb seeds or beans), empty 2-litre plastic bottle

Method: You will need an adult to help you to cut.

1. Cut the bottom off a large plastic drink bottle.
2. Plant the seeds in your school garden and place the plastic bottle over some of them.
3. Leave some seeds uncovered, so that you can compare their growth with the seeds under the mini greenhouse.

Activities

A. Answer the Questions.

1. What object would you use to measure temperature?
2. What scale do we use to measure temperature in degrees?
3. At what temperature does water boil?
4. At what temperature does water freeze?
5. Name three places where you might find a thermometer.
6. What happens to air when it is heated?

B: Think About It.

1. Describe the ways in which each of the following animals stays cool.

   (a) snake, **(b)** dog, **(c)** elephant, **(d)** crocodile

2. Describe the things that humans do to stay cool.

Subject:	Science	Strand:	Energy and Forces / Materials
Strand Unit:	Heat (linked to Materials and Change)		

Subject:	Geography	Strand:	Natural Environments
Strand Unit:	Weather, Climate and Atmosphere		

Unit 18: Materials

WHAT ARE YOU MAKING WITH ALL THAT CARDBOARD?

A COOL NEW DOG HOUSE FOR THE BACK GARDEN.

I DON'T THINK THAT CARDBOARD IS A GOOD MATERIAL TO USE FOR A DOG HOUSE! WHAT WILL HAPPEN WHEN IT RAINS?

IT'LL BE A COOL DOG HOUSE ALRIGHT; ESPECIALLY ON A WINDY NIGHT!

Materials

When we hear the word 'material', we usually think about what our clothes, cushions or curtains are made from. In science, the word 'material' is used to describe what an object is made from. For example, the window is made from glass; the door is made from wood; the bag is made from leather. Glass, wood and leather are materials. Materials are chosen because they are good for doing a certain job. Glass is a good material for windows, because we can see through it.

Chairs

What kind of chair are you sitting in? Which of the chairs above would you like to sit in? What is each chair made from? Do you remember Goldilocks? She was very fussy about the kind of chair that she wanted to sit in: not too big; not too small; but just right. You will sit in lots of chairs during your lifetime. Are all the chairs in your house or school made from the same materials? What is your favourite chair?

All chairs have something in common. A chair is a piece of furniture with a raised surface, so that you can sit up off the floor. Chairs are designed to support the human body. There are many different kinds of chair and many different materials are used to make them. Look at the chairs on the right. Do you think the materials used are suitable?

Chair made from grass and soil

Chair made from ice

Chair made from cardboard

Subject:	Science	**Strand:**	Materials
Strand Unit:	Properties and Characteristics of Materials

Subject:	Geography	**Strand:**	Human Environments
Strand Unit:	People Living and Working in a Local Area

105

Materials Around the House

Nineteenth-century Kitchen

Look at the photographs of a modern kitchen and a kitchen from the nineteenth century. Many of the materials used to build kitchens have changed. A modern kitchen has many

Modern Kitchen

appliances made from aluminium and stainless steel. Appliances were first produced from those materials early in the 1900s. Cast iron, tin, copper and stone appliances were used in kitchens before that time.

Materials for Building Houses

In Ireland, we mostly use concrete blocks and wood to build houses. However, many other materials are used around the world. Materials are chosen because they are available nearby, people can afford them and they are suited to the natural environment. Look at the following houses from different parts of the world.

In Canada many houses are made from vinyl and other unnatural, or synthetic, materials. They are delivered, ready-made, by lorry.	Nomads of the Gobi Desert in Asia make houses covered in layered cloth. The layers are filled with animal wool and hair.	In Morocco, houses are built from sun-dried clay bricks. The bricks help to keep the temperature cool inside the house.

Activities

A. Answer the Questions.

1. Why is cardboard not a good material for a dog house?
2. Why do we use chairs?
3. List the materials from which your class chair is made.
4. What does 'material' mean in science?
5. Name two materials from which windows are made.
6. Name two appliances in your kitchen that are made from stainless steel.
7. Name two appliances in your kitchen that are made from plastic.

B. Write the Materials Used to Build Each of the Following.

1. igloo, 2. tepee, 3. forest cabin, 4. Irish cottage, 5. greenhouse, 6. caravan

Subject:	Science	Strand:	Materials
Strand Unit:	Properties and Characteristics of Materials		

Subject:	Geography	Strand:	Human Environments
Strand Unit:	People Living and Working in a Local Area		

C. Think About It.

Modern Irish house

Nineteenth-century Irish cottage

1. Look at the photographs above. In what ways are the two houses similar?
2. In what ways are the two houses different?
3. Were the homes of long ago built from the same materials as the homes of today?

Raw Materials

Most materials are rarely used in their natural, or raw, form. They usually go through a manufacturing process before we use them. Wood comes from trees. It is a natural material. It is cut, sanded and oiled before it is made into furniture. Gemstones are a natural material, but they must be cut and polished before being made into jewellery. Wool from a sheep is treated and dyed before it is woven into material for clothes. Cotton, paper, wood and silk are all natural materials.

Silkworm cocoon

Cotton plant

Raw wool

Glass is made from heated sand, which is a natural material. However, most of the glass that we see had other materials added to it during the manufacturing process.

Raw metals are found in rocks, where they are usually mixed with pieces of rock and other materials. The rocks are heated until the raw metal melts and flows out. This way of getting metal from rocks is known as smelting.

Smelting iron

Some materials, such as plastic, are made from chemicals. They are known as synthetic materials.

Metal Fact File

- The Earth's core contains lots of iron.

- Aluminum is the most common metal found in the Earth's crust (the outer layer of the Earth).

Earth's crust

- Many metals can be melted at high temperatures and then shaped to make various objects.

- Metals can be mixed together. An alloy is a mixture of two or more metals.

- Electricity and heat travel easily through most metals.

Plastic Fact File

- Plastic is not found naturally. However, it is made from wood or oil.

- Cellophane and ping-pong balls are made of plastic made from wood.

- Polystyrene, PVC, nylon and acrylic are types of plastic that come from oil.

- There are thousands of types of plastic.

- Plastic is harmful to the environment and it is difficult to recycle.

- Electricity will not travel through plastic.

WILL THIS CARRIER BAG BREAK BECAUSE OF THE WEIGHT OF MY SHOPPING?

WILL THIS SCHOOLBAG BE STRONG ENOUGH TO HOLD ALL OF MY BOOKS?

WILL THIS COAT KEEP ME DRY IN THE RAIN?

Choosing Materials

You make decisions about materials every day. To choose the most suitable material, you must think about the job that you want it to do. If you are choosing the best cloth to mop up a spill, you will think about how much liquid the cloth can soak up. To choose the best ball for a certain sport, you will think about how well it bounces. The best gym shoes should bend easily instead of being stiff. Some materials can be judged just by looking at them, but others need more investigation.

Hot Geography

About 380 billion plastic bags are used in the USA each year. That is more than 1200 bags per person. In Ireland, we were using 328 plastic shopping bags per person each year up until 2002. Since 2002, we have to pay for every plastic bag we use. The number of bags that we use has dropped to 21 bags per person each year.

Investigate: Which Material Makes the Bounciest Ball?

You will need: A rubber ball, plasticine ball, sponge ball, tennis ball

Method:

1. Drop each ball and observe how far it bounces back up.

2. Remember to keep the test fair by dropping the balls from the same height onto the same surface.

Test:

- Is it fair to throw the ball instead of dropping it?

Subject:	Science	Strand:	Materials
Strand Unit:	Properties and Characteristics of Materials		

Subject:	Geography	Strand:	Human Environments
Strand Unit:	People Living and Working in a Local Area		

Investigate: Which Material Makes the Strongest Hanger?

You will need: Metal hanger, wooden hanger, plastic hanger

Method: Hang weights on the hangers to find out which is the strongest.

  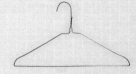

Investigate: Are Materials Waterproof?

You will need: Paper bag, plastic bag, fabric bag

Method: Design a test to investigate whether or not each bag is waterproof.

Activities

A. Answer the Questions.

1. Name three metals.
2. Name three types of plastic.
3. What is the most common metal found in the Earth's crust?
4. What metals are used to make euro coins?
5. From what raw material is nylon made?

B. Write the Following Materials in Order, Starting With the Strongest.

cardboard, tissue, kitchen roll, copy paper, a birthday card

C. Find the Meaning of the Following Words in Your Dictionary.

1. natural, **2.** manufactured, **3.** synthetic, **4.** alloy, **5.** absorbent

D. Think About It.

London Bridge   London Tower Bridge   Golden Gate Bridge, San Francisco

1. Look at photographs of famous bridges above. **(a)** What materials were used to build the bridges? **(b)** Which shape do you think makes the strongest bridge?

2. Make a bridge using only two pieces of A4 paper. Place the bridge between two 'pillars' of books (you cannot use anything else to hold the bridge). Test your bridge design by placing coins or toy cars on top. (The best design will hold the most weight.)

E. Digging Deeper.

Find out about a bridge in your local area. Draw a picture of it and write about the materials from which it is made.

| Subject: | Science | Strand: | Materials | | Subject: | Geography | Strand: | Human Environments |
| Strand Unit: | Properties and Characteristics of Materials | | | | Strand Unit: | People Living and Working in a Local Area | | |

109

Unit 19: Weather

Weather Is Important

IT LOOKS LIKE IT WILL RAIN.

THE WEATHER FORECAST SAYS THAT IT WILL BE DRY TODAY.

WE HAVE NO WAY OF KNOWING WHAT THE WEATHER WILL BE LIKE.

The weather is a very important part of our daily lives. It helps us to decide what clothes to wear, what activities we can do and to where we will go on holidays. Knowledge of weather is important for all of us, but it is especially important for farmers, fishermen and pilots. They have to plan their work around the weather and avoid bad weather for safety reasons. In some parts of the world, people worry about the weather as there can be hurricanes, droughts, tornadoes, tropical storms and even ice storms!

Tornado

WHAT DANGERS/DAMAGE DO THESE WEATHER CONDITIONS CAUSE?

Flood

Drought

Hurricane

Snow

What Makes Up Weather?

Weather is made up of various things, including temperature, cloud cover, rainfall and wind direction and speed. Often when we talk about weather, we are describing how the sun, rain and wind work together and affect our lives.

Temperature

Temperature is a measure of how hot or cold something is. We use a thermometer to record the temperature in an area.

Thermometer

Hot Geography

The study of weather is called meteorology. The people who study it are called meteorologists. There are several weather stations in Ireland. The Met Éireann headquarters are in Dublin. Take a look at the weather tonight after the news.

| Subject: | Geography | Strand: | Natural Environments |
| Strand Unit: | Weather, Climate and Atmosphere | | |

| Subject: | Science | Strand: | Environmental Awareness and Care |
| Strand Unit: | Environmental Awareness | | |

Wind

Wind is moving air that travels from one place to another. It brings heat and moisture from the place where it has just been, to the place where it is going. Moisture means the amount of water that is in the air. Winds are named after the direction from which they have come.

Westerly

Winds that travel from North America to Ireland are known as westerly winds, as they travel from the west.

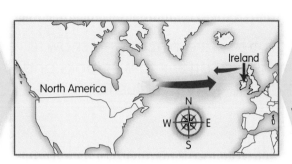

Easterly

Winds that travel from Central Europe to Ireland are known as easterly winds, as they travel from the east.

Westerly winds usually bring cool and wet weather. This is because of the moisture that they pick up over the Atlantic Ocean. Northerly winds bring cold, harsh and bitter weather. This is because they travel from the North Pole. Southerly winds bring warm, mild weather, as they travel from the equator. Easterly winds bring snow, frost and fog, as they travel from Russia and Siberia.

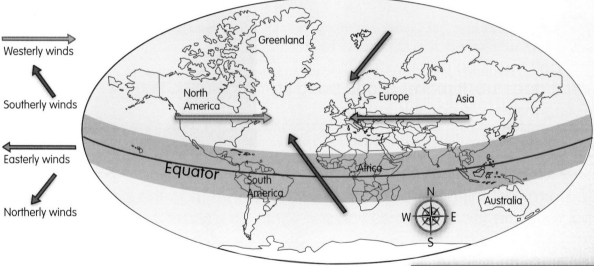

Rain

The wind often brings rain with it, but it depends on the direction it has travelled from. When the sun shines, it heats the water in the rivers, streams, lakes and sea. The water turns into steam, or water vapour, and rises into the sky. The water vapour then cools into droplets that form a cloud. When there are too many droplets in the cloud, the water falls to the ground as rain. A rainbow is formed when the sun shines through water droplets in the air. We usually see rainbows in the sky when there are rain showers.

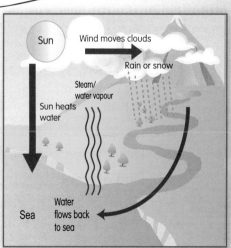

Hail

Hail

Hail is frozen rain. Hailstones are usually about the size of a pea, but some larger hailstones can be as big as a tennis ball. Next time it hails, watch out!

Sleet

Sleet is a mixture of rain and snow. It melts quickly after it falls. It looks and feels a little bit like a 'slushie'.

Sleet

Snow

When the water in a cloud becomes very cold, the droplets of water freeze, forming snow crystals. Snow crystals fall to the ground as snowflakes. The temperature must be 0 °C or lower for the snowflake to stick to the ground. If not, it will melt and turn into water.

Hot History

The Greeks fenced off spots that had been struck by lightning so that humans would not walk on ground touched by the gods.

KEEP OUT

Snow crystal

Thunder

Thunder is formed when the air close to a lightning bolt heats up quickly and then cools. As it does this, it makes a loud banging or rumbling noise. We call this thunder.

Lightning

Lightning

Lightning is the large electrical spark that comes from a cloud during a thunderstorm. Lightning is more than five times hotter than the surface of the sun. Light travels faster than sound, so you see lightning before you hear the sound of thunder. Lightning can strike people and buildings, so it is really important to stay safe during a thunderstorm. Stay away from trees, water, windows and doors. If you are outside, try to make your way indoors as quickly as possible.

Activities

1. Name three things that make up the weather.
2. What do we use to measure temperature?
3. What kind of weather comes with northerly winds?
4. What kind of weather comes with southerly winds?
5. Write three sentences to explain how the weather affects each of the following people:
   (a) farmer, (b) fisherman, (c) pilot, (d) holiday maker, (e) cyclist

Subject:	Geography	Strand:	Natural Environments
Strand Unit:	Weather, Climate and Atmosphere		

Subject:	Science	Strand:	Environmental Awareness and Care
Strand Unit:	Environmental Awareness		

6. Meteorologists study the weather using images that are taken by satellites in space. Look at the satellite image and the map below. Write **(a)** two things that are the same about the satellite image and the map and **(b)** two things that are different.

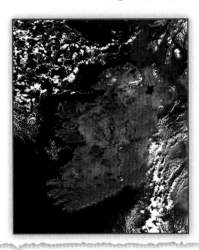

Clouds

There can be lots of different types of cloud in the sky over Ireland. Some of the clouds are soft and puffy like candy floss. Others are long and wispy like pieces of thread. Some can be dark, grey and angry-looking. Clouds move with the wind. Clouds have different names depending on how high they are in the sky. Different types of cloud come with different types of weather. By watching the movement of the clouds, we can tell from which direction the weather is travelling. If we did not have clouds, we would not have rain, hail, sleet or snow! The four main types of cloud are cirrus, alto, stratus and cumulus.

Cirrus clouds are the most common type of high cloud. They are made from ice and are long, thin and wispy. Cirrus clouds are usually white and they come with fair and pleasant weather.

Cirrus

Alto

Alto clouds are found in the middle level of the sky. They are made up of water droplets and are usually grey in colour. They are soft and puffy and stretch out in waves across the sky. Alto clouds often carry heavy rain.

Stratus clouds are fluffy and usually stretch across the entire sky. These clouds are grey in colour and can look like fog. Stratus clouds usually bring drizzle and mist.

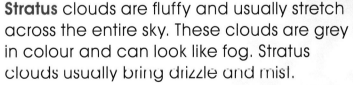
Stratus

Cumulus

Cumulus clouds are soft, fluffy clouds that look like balls of cotton wool floating across the sky. Cumulus clouds usually lie low in the sky and come with fair to good weather.

Investigate: How Much Rain Falls in Your Playground?

You will need: An empty 2-litre plastic bottle, scissors, sticky tape, ruler

Method: With a partner, make your own rain gauge.

1. Draw a sketch of what you want your rain gauge to look like.
2. Cut the top third off the plastic bottle and remove it.
3. Turn the top of the bottle upside-down and fit it into the bottom part. Use sticky tape to keep it in place.
4. Place the ruler along the side of your rain gauge and use sticky tape to keep it in place. The amount of rainfall is measured in millimetres.
5. Find a suitable place in the playground, for example, a flower-bed. Dig a hollow in the ground and place the rain gauge into it. This will stop the rain gauge from falling over.
6. Remember to check the rain gauge every day and record your results on the record sheet in your Activity Book.

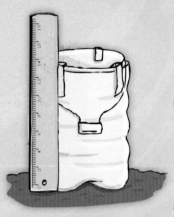

Activities

A. Answer the Questions.

1. What is the difference between hail, sleet and snow?
2. What is the difference between alto clouds and cumulus clouds?
3. Look outside your window. **(a)** What type of clouds are in the sky? **(b)** What kind of weather does this type of cloud usually come with?

B. Draw a Diagram (Picture) and Explain How Rain Is Formed.

C. Look at the Map on Page 28. Use the Maps Below to Write the Weather Forecast for Your Area on Wednesday and Sunday.

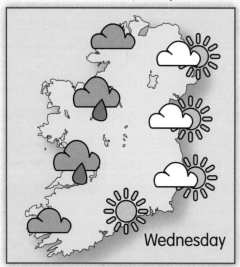

Wednesday

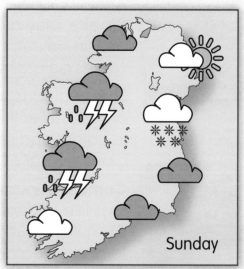

Sunday

Subject: Geography **Strand:** Natural Environments
Strand Unit: Weather, Climate and Atmosphere

Subject: Science **Strand:** Environmental Awareness and Care
Strand Unit: Environmental Awareness

 # Unit 20: Soils

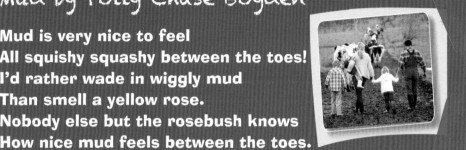

Mud by Polly Chase Boyden

Mud is very nice to feel
All squishy squashy between the toes!
I'd rather wade in wiggly mud
Than smell a yellow rose.
Nobody else but the rosebush knows
How nice mud feels between the toes.

How Is Soil Made?

Wind, water and ice break rocks into little pieces. Heat, water, pressure and chemicals change the rock pieces.

⬇

Small plants start to grow in the broken rock pieces. Their roots break down the rocks even more.

⬇

The plants die and start to rot over the rock pieces. This forms soil. Larger plants start to grow.

⬇

Animals and mini-beasts start to live in the plants and the soil. They die and rot into the soil, making it even richer. More plants grow. Most soil has taken thousands of years to form. Soils can come in lots of colours: black, red, yellow, white, brown and grey.

From What Is Soil Made?

Soil is one of the most important materials on our planet. It is like a living skin that covers the surface of the Earth. Soil is made up of a mixture of living and non-living materials. It is made from rocks, plants and animals that have broken down into smaller pieces over time. Sand is made only from rocks that have broken down into tiny pieces. Soil contains clay, sand, gravel, humus (decaying plant and animal remains), air spaces and water. Soil helps to support plants by giving them nutrients (food), water, and air. Soil also keeps the plants' roots in the ground so that they can grow upright, towards the sunlight.

 ## Investigate: What Is in Soil?

You will need: Sieve, magnifying glass, soil sample

Method: Use a sieve and a magnifying glass to find out what is in your soil sample. Can you find any pieces of rocks, or living or dead plants or animals?

Yellow desert soil

Living Things in Soil

Soil is home to many underground animals and insects, including the earthworm, ant and mole. Soil also contains micro-organisms such as bacteria, fungi and lichens. Many of these can only be seen with a magnifying glass or a microscope.

Ant

Mole and earthworm

The most common creature in soil is the earthworm. Earthworms create tunnels in the soil, helping air and water to move through the soil. They also eat rotting plant materials, which pass through their bodies and fertilise the soil. Larger animals such as mice and moles dig burrows that also bring air into the soil. Air pockets allow the animals that live in the soil to breathe.

Investigate: What Kind of Soil Is in Your Area?

You will need: Soil sample

Method: Collect a sample of soil from around your school or in your own garden. Squeeze some of the soil between your fingers.

- How does it feel?
- Is it crumbly or sticky?
- Are there big pieces in it or small grains?
- What colour is it?
- Can you find any living things in it? Do you see any pieces of rotting plants in it?
- Record what you have found out in your science copy.

Common Soil Types in Ireland

Clay

Loam

Sandy soil

Silt

Subject:	Geography	Strand:	Natural Environments
Strand Unit:	Rocks and Soils		

Subject:	Science	Strand:	Living Things
Strand Unit:	Plants and Animals		

The most common types of soil in Ireland are sandy soil, clay, silt and loam. If the soil crumbles and falls apart, it is probably sandy soil. If you can squeeze it into shapes, it is clay. Clay feels sticky when it is wet. Loam is a mixture of sandy soil and clay. Loam is the best soil for growing most plants. Silt is a very fine, dusty soil that is found near rivers. It is left behind by a river after it has flooded and the water level has returned to normal.

The type of soil in an area affects the types of plants and animals that live there. Farmers and gardeners must know the type of soil that they have in order to decide what plants and crops will grow best. If the soil is not suitable, certain plants will not grow well and may even die.

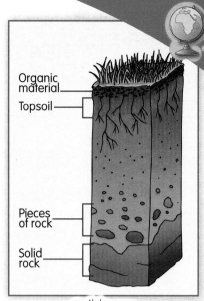

Organic material
Topsoil
Pieces of rock
Solid rock

Soil layers

Activities

A. Choose the Correct Answer to Complete Each Sentence.

1. Soil contains _____.
   (a) living things, **(b)** dead things, or **(c)** living and non-living things

2. Sand is made only from _____.
   (a) soil, **(b)** mud, or **(c)** rocks

3. Humus is _____.
   (a) decayed plants and animals, **(b)** a funny story, or **(c)** a bone in your arm

4. The best soil for growing most plants is _____.
   (a) sand, **(b)** no soil, or **(c)** loam

B. Fill in the Missing Words.

1. The most common living creature in the soil is the _____.

2. Soil contains millions of micro-_____ such as bacteria and fungi.

3. The food for plants in soil is called _____.

4. Soil holds the plants' _____ in the ground.

5. Earthworms eat _____ plant materials.

C. Get Creative.

1. Write a diary page for a mole. Write about all the creatures he meets in the soil (mice, earthworms and mini-beasts).

2. Write your own poem called 'Mud'.

How Does Water Get into Soil?

When it rains, water soaks into the spaces between the particles (small pieces) in the soil. The roots of plants soak up the extra water. When there is very little rainfall, the roots of the plants help to suck the water down into the soil.

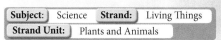

Investigate: How Much Water Is in Soil?

You will need: Plastic container, soil sample, weighing scales, cling film

Method:

1. Place your soil sample in the plastic container and weigh it.
2. Leave the container of soil in a warm place on a windowsill or near a radiator for a number of days.
3. Weigh it again. Has there been a change? Why?
4. Wrap the container of soil with cling film and return it to the windowsill for a few days. What do you notice? Where do the drops of water come from?
5. Record what you have found out in your science copy.

Mudslides

After a wildfire or a drought, soil can be blown away or washed away when there are no plants to hold it in place. Mudslides happen when there is too much rainfall on loose soil, or as a result of an earthquake. They happen suddenly, often without warning and may result in the loss of life. Read the following news report about a mudslide that occured in 2011.

The number of people killed following the mudslides north of Rio de Janeiro rose to 464 on Thursday. Survivors of the disaster struggled to reach their neighbours, who were trapped under layers of mud. Wednesday's mudslides in the mountainous region destroyed homes and businesses and swept away cars and trucks. Roads and bridges were also washed away, making it impossible for emergency vehicles to reach the area. Survivors had to dig through the mud with shovels and bare hands.

Why is Soil So Important?

- Soil can hold lots of water and prevent flooding.

- Most of our food grows in soil. The rest comes from animals that eat plants that grow in soil. Without soil we would not have any food.

- Many antibiotics are made from micro-organisms that live in soil.

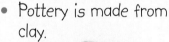

- Pottery is made from clay.

- These houses in Iceland are made using sods of soil and grass!

Subject:	Geography	Strand:	Natural Environments
Strand Unit:	Rocks and Soils		

Subject:	Science	Strand:	Living Things
Strand Unit:	Plants and Animals		

Hot Geography

NASA's Mars rover *Curiosity* found soil that looks very like the volcanic sand in Hawaii, scientists say.

Surface of Mars

The Surface of Mars

Mars is the fourth planet from the sun. It has hard, rocky land that you could walk on. Mars is dry and much of it is covered with reddish dust and rocks. It often has huge dust-storms with high-speed winds. The duststorms are made by the sun. Dust is sent far up into space, covering much of the planet of Mars. Some storms can be seen by people using telescopes on Earth. Mars is smaller than Earth and it is much colder. There is evidence that there was once water on Mars. If people were ever to live on Mars, they would need to find a way to turn the red dust into fertile soil.

Activities

A. Answer True or False. Write the False Sentences Correctly.

1. Soil is always the exact same colour.
2. Sand is made only from tiny pieces of rock.
3. Sandy soil feels sticky when it's wet.
4. Pottery is made from silt.
5. Earthworms make tunnels in the soil.
6. Humans do not use soil.

B. Answer the Following Questions.

1. Name three types of soil.
2. What is soil made from?
3. How do humans use soil?
4. Name three animals that live in soil.
5. What part of a plant helps to hold it in place in the soil?
6. What is the top layer of soil called?

C. Think About It.

1. Why is soil good for plants?
2. Why is the earthworm good for the soil?
3. What is underneath the soil?
4. How could you prevent a mudslide from happening?
5. Do you think humans could live on Mars?
6. How do humans damage soil?

| **Subject:** Geography | **Strand:** Natural Environments | **Subject:** Science | **Strand:** Living Things |
| **Strand Unit:** Rocks and Soils | | **Strand Unit:** Plants and Animals | |

119

Glossary

Altitude (Unit 8): Height above sea level

Bedouin (Unit 11): People of the desert in North Africa

Canopy (Unit 12): Highest layer or roof of trees and branches in the rainforest

Carnivore (Unit 1): Animal that eats other animals

Cartilage (Unit 14): Soft material like bone, found in parts of the body such as your ear

Circuit (Unit 15): Circle of power, wires and bulb (or other appliance) that carries electricity

Colony (Unit 4): People or animals who work together

Communicate (Unit 6): Share news or information with others

Community (Units 2 and 4): People who live or work in an area

Commute (Unit 5): Travel to and from work or school

Conductor (Unit 15): Something that allows electricity (or heat) to pass through

Council (Unit 4): Paid workers who make your community cleaner, safer and better

Crust (Unit 8): Outer layer of the Earth, on which we live

Decibels (Unit 13): Units used to measure how loud a sound is

Enamel (Unit 14): Very strong material found in your teeth

Environment (Unit 7): Place or conditions in which people, plants or animals live

Equator (Unit 12): Horizontal line on a map that divides the world in two halves

Fertilise (Units 3 and 20): Add 'food' such as compost or manure to soil

Food pyramid (Unit 14): Chart that guides us towards healthy food

Friction (Unit 17): Rubbing things together to create heat

Galaxy (Unit 16): Huge collection of stars

Government (Unit 9): People who govern or run a country

Herbivore (Unit 1): Animal that eats plants

Humus (Unit 20): Remains of plants or animals that have rotted

Independent country (Unit 9): Country that is not ruled by another country

Insulator (Unit 15): Something that does not allow electricity (or heat) to pass through

Islam (Unit 11): Religion of Muslims

Joint (Unit 14): Place such as the elbow where bones meet

Magma (Unit 8 and 17): Hot liquid rock inside the Earth

Manufacture (Unit 18): Make something, usually in a factory

Meteorology (Unit 19): The science of weather

Micro-organisms (Unit 20): Tiny living creatures such as bacteria

Omnivore (Unit 1): Animal that eats plants and animals

Online (Unit 6): Connected to the internet

Organic (Unit 20): Living or once living

Oxygen (Unit 3): Very important gas in the air we breathe

Parliament (Unit 9): Elected people who make a country's laws

Rainforests (Unit 12): Wet jungles or forests found in hot parts of the world

Ramadan (Unit 11): Special time of the year for Muslims

Reservoir (Unit 2): Natural or man-made lake

Rural (Unit 5): To do with country life

Solar system (Unit 16): Group of planets, asteroids and comets that spin around a sun

Suburb (Unit 5): Area with lots of houses on the edge of a city

Synthetic (Unit 18): Man-made, not natural

Technology (Unit 10): Making science useful

Thermometer (Unit 17): Instrument used to tell how hot something is (its temperature)

Transmit (Unit 10): Send a message, usually as a radio or televison signal

Urban (Unit 5): To do with city or town life

Vibrate (Unit 13): Shake – sound waves make your eardrum vibrate

Water vapour (Unit 19): Water that has evaporated (turned to steam)